the story of
Stereophonics

First Published in 1999 by
INDEPENDENT MUSIC PRESS LTD.
This Edition Published by Independent Music Press in 2002
This Work is Copyright © Independent Music Press Ltd 1999

High Times & Headlines - The Story of Stereophonics
by Mike Black

British Library Cataloguing-in-Publication Data.
A catalogue for this book is available from The British Library.
ISBN 1-89-7783-18-3

Every effort has been made to contact the photographers whose
work has been used in this book - however a few were unobtainable.
The publishers would be grateful if those concerned would contact
Independent Music Press Ltd.

Cover & book design by Philip Gambrill.
Printed and bound in Ireland.

PICTURE CREDITS:

B/W Photo Credits (in page order): 8: Rex Features; 13: Angela Lubrano/Live; 17: Anna
Meuer/SIN; 22, 29 & 32: Martyn Goodacre/SIN; 39: Ray Tang/Rex Features; 42: Suzan
Moore/All Action; 44: David Hardacre/SIN; 48: Justin Thomas/All Action; 52: David
Hardacre/SIN; 56: Tim Auger/Retna; 60 & 66: David Hardacre/SIN; 72 Brian Rasic/Rex
Features; 78: Martyn Goodacre/Retna; 83: Roger Sargent/Rex Features; 84: Rob
Watkins/Retna; 89: Angela Lubrano/Live; 95: David Hardacre/SIN; 98: Piers Allardyce/SIN;
105 & 110: Angela Lubrano/Live; 113: Rob Watkins/Retna; 117: Martyn Goodacre/Retna;
120 & 125: David Hardacre/SIN; 125; 131: Andy Wilsher/SIN; 135: Angela Lubrano/Live
Colour Section (in order): E Catarina/Retna; Martyn Goodacre/SIN;
Rex Features; David Hardacre/SIN; David Hardacre/SIN; Paul Meaker/All Action;
Angela Lubrano/Live; Martyn Goodacre/SIN.

INDEPENDENT MUSIC PRESS
P.O. Box 14691
London
SE1 2ZA

Web: www.impbooks.com
E-mail: info@impbooks.com
Fax: 020 7357 8608

the story of
Stereophonics

by

Mike Black

Independent Music Press
London

Thanks and acknowledgements to the journalists of
the following publications whose sterling coverage of Stereophonics'
career was of inestimable value in putting together this,
the first complete history of the band:

Billboard, The Guardian, Kerrang!, Making Music, Melody Maker,
Music Week, NME, Q, Rock Sound, Select, Smash Hits, Vox,
plus sundry Stereophonics websites, official and otherwise.

1 Stuart Bailie *Melody Maker* 2 Feb 77
2 Jake Barnes *Music Week* Nov 96
3 Simon Williams *NME* 24 Jan 98
4 Dan Gennoe *Making Music* Nov 98
5 Mark Griffiths *Kerrang* Aug 99
6 Ben Myers *Kerrang* May 99
7 Neil Madson *Melody Maker* 7 Aug 99
8 paul *Sexton Billboard* Aug 99
9 Ben Myers *Melody Maker* 20 Feb 99
10 Sam Upton *Select* Feb 99

Contents

the story of Stereophonics

INTRODUCTION

The organisers of a radio survey tuned into the five main stations serving London in August 1999, their purpose to find out the breadth of music the capital's listeners were being offered. Interestingly, two out of those five – Capital, the biggest independent station in Britain, and XFM, London's self-proclaimed alternative music outlet – were playing the Stereophonics.

It might not have been statistically sound, but this straw poll gave some indication of the all-pervasive power of the Welsh trio's music as the millennium approached. From a standing start three years earlier, they'd produced two acclaimed albums, notched a string of hit singles without losing credibility with the 'indie-rock' audience and put Richard Branson's V2 record label – to whom they were the first signings – firmly on the musical map.

Yet this was no manufactured success story. The Stereophonics had based their success on stage savvy beyond their years, nurtured in the pubs, social clubs and railmen's institutes of their native South Wales. Playing to an audience ranging in age from 9-90 and in attitude from indifferent to downright hostile, they learned early on how to entertain. That love of playing live has never left them. 'We're the type of band that tours 11 months of the year,' explains guitarist Kelly Jones. 'It's cheaper than therapy.'

Almost every outdoor rock event you could visit in 1997 and 1998 featured Kelly, unrelated bassist Richard Jones and drummer Stuart Cable, all three ready and willing to convert those festival-goers attracted by bigger names. By 1999, and with a chart-topping second album,

Performance And Cocktails, behind them, there was little need to steal others' fans: the Stereophonics were themselves the big draw. They proved it, too, with a July 1999 concert in Swansea: 50,000 fans crammed into the crumbling Morfa athletics stadium, with thousands more unable to obtain a ticket.

The small-town upbringing they shared in Cwmaman, a former pit village, gave Kelly Jones his early inspiration, and perhaps it's this – along with their championing of the Welsh rugby team – that's led their fans to adopt the national flag as their own. Certainly, the rise of the Manic Street Preachers, Catatonia, Super Furry Animals and other bands from the Principality did the Stereophonics no harm. Yet the band are much more than merely local heroes, and their travels since the 1997 release of their first album, *Word Gets Around*, have noticeably widened their lyrical worldview.

Musical categories, too, have fallen in the face of the Phonics onslaught. It's no surprise, for instance, that heavy-metal weekly magazine *Kerrang!* has been among the trio's biggest supporters. The band's no-nonsense, 'neighbourhood gang' image – plus Richard's tattoos and a collective love of veteran Australian metallurgists AC/DC – have been enough to endear them to fans of wilder, heavier outfits, while *Melody Maker*'s similar championing has proved they retain their street-level rock cred. But no band since the Jam have managed to ally this with a string of hit singles that lodge in the memory like dumdum bullets, Jones' incisive lyricism matched by music that rarely outstays its welcome. Not for this band the lazy 'ad lib and fade' attitude of some big names we could mention: Stereophonics songs typically make their point in around three minutes, making them obvious aforementioned radio staples.

By seemingly ignoring image, presenting their music in a simple, unvarnished format and working their backsides off on the live music circuit, the Stereophonics appear to have become the least likely superstars of the 1990s. Exactly what they will achieve in the new millennium can only be imagined, but it seems conceivable that, should they conquer America at the second time of asking, they will have the known rock world at their feet. Not bad work for an extrovert who used to deliver school dinners, a spiritually aware former school ruffian and a trainee scriptwriter who turned his hand to the common pop song…

Mike Black
September 1999

chapter 1:

THE MORFA EXPERIENCE

It was to be the gig to end all gigs. On 23 February 1999, Stereophonics proudly announced that, as well as several other festival appearances planned for the coming summer, they'd be headlining their very own rock'n'roll party. The outdoor event at the Morfa Stadium in Swansea at the end of July was the nearest they'd come to playing home turf, as a band spokesman noted.

'The Stereophonics were keen to stage a major event in Swansea, a city which they feel they have previously overlooked on their live schedule. They chose the more urban site of Morfa Stadium, built over the site of the original steel works, as it has always had strong links with the working people of Swansea and South Wales, often depicted in the songs of Kelly Jones.' The singer himself was rather more down to earth about the choice, giving class solidarity the slip and preferring to liken his band to a popular low-fat spread! 'We played in Cardiff Castle last year, that's why we're playing Swansea this year. We like to spread ourselves around. Like Flora…'

What's more, this would be the venue's swansong; Swansea City Football Club had earmarked the site for the building of a new all-seater stadium, and the next thing to be heard after the Phonics had vacated the stage would be the sound of onrushing bulldozers... not that many acts would fancy following the Stereophonics in current form.

The supporting bill of special guests and side attractions for the 31 July show took shape in the coming weeks and would offer something for everyone, while tickets priced at a more than reasonable £19.50 for the day were snapped up in record time. Regardless of whether the support had been the Nolans, Showaddywaddy and Steps or the re-formed Led Zeppelin (dream on), it was clear this would be the biggest live music event to be staged in South Wales. Ever.

'Probably just right for a spot of housebreaking, I reckon... the whole place must be deserted.'

Quite how big, though, was open to question. By March, 25,000 tickets had passed across the counter and it was a question of how 'elastic' Morfa's ancient walls could possibly be. A Stereophonics spokesman commented, 'The sky's the limit in terms of the number of tickets they can sell in Wales.' At that point, the upper limit had been set at 35,000, but this would eventually stretch to 50,000 – though the boys apparently hadn't been keen on their management asking for an extension in case they seemed big-headed!

The Stereophonics were making sure that the Morfa Stadium would retire with due ceremony. Having hosted many major sporting competitions in the previous two decades, it was planned to include a programme of Pro-Celebrity events as part of the day's activities. A fairground with rides was doing good business in one corner of the ground, while a memorabilia auction would also be held with all proceeds going to charity. If Catatonia hadn't already copyrighted the line, it would have been a day to 'wake up and thank the Lord you were Welsh...'

The turnout was both loud and large, with three coach-loads of fans arriving from the band's home town of Cwmaman alone. This, drummer Stuart Cable helpfully remarked as the day dawned, meant the time was 'probably just right for a spot of housebreaking, I reckon... the whole place must be *deserted*.' Was he nervous at the prospect of topping such a bill at such a venue? 'Good God, yes!' came the typically forthright reply. 'There are just so many people here.' He wasn't wrong.

To put the scale of Morfa into perspective, the Phonics would be playing to five times as many people as they had at the previous year's triumphant Cardiff Castle gig. But one thing they wouldn't be playing in was a five-a-side football competition featuring an impressive number of past sports stars. The roll call included recently retired Welsh soccer international Ian Rush, world champion boxer Joe Calzaghe and national rugby heroes Ieuan Evans and Gareth Davies. Musicians were allowed to participate too, but with three notable exceptions: 'The insurance company wouldn't let us,' moaned Kelly.

Support band Reef were seemingly unrestrained by such contractual small print – and proved it when their green-shirted team won the event with guitarist Kenwyn House and drummer Dominic Greensmith both writing their names on the scoresheet in the final. They held the small trophy (which some careless person had earlier broken) aloft with pride... and, for once, the Phonics could only look on with envy...

The eagerly contested round-ball event had been preceded by a tug of war, a spectacle rarely seen outside village greens of several years ago, that played to local rivalry by pitching together the muscled men of the Cardiff and Swansea rugby clubs. It was followed by the erection of a boxing ring which would stage three fights between local hopefuls as the 'undercard' to a bout between five times Welsh champion Leighton Godrich and Welsh international Andrew Campbell. For the record, it was Godrich who came out with arm raised high.

The moving force behind the event was Kelly, who'd been something of a star pugilist in his youth. 'Amateur boxing clubs in Wales are always skint,' he'd explained beforehand, 'and it's a good way of them raising money. I've never seen one of those at a festival before... but no, I won't be fighting.' The Llansamlet Boxing Club were the beneficiaries as we were treated to the unusual sight of a usually peace-loving concert crowd baying for blood.

Proceedings kicked off, musically speaking, with a band most of the assembled 50,000 would recognise just as quickly as they would the headliners. Well, at first glance, anyway... There were absolutely no prizes for guessing who AB/CD were attempting to pay tribute to, and they proved an inspired choice to warm up the crowd with some lowest common denominator anthems delivered in tongue-in-cheek style.

Whether you liked the originals or not, this band was loud, proud and, above all, realistic. 'The guitarist even looked like Angus when he took his shirt off,' was Stuart's approving comment from the wings as the Gibson SG-toting 'schoolboy' proved he had Master Young's riffs down to a T. Little wonder, then, that one of the St John's Ambulancemen present to deal with cases of sunstroke – and there were several – was heard to opine that the band were the only tribute outfit to have AC-DC's official blessing!

The fans were already enjoying themselves, among them former Page 3 model-turned-TV presenter Melinda Messenger. 'I'm a very big fan of the Stereophonics,' she told *Melody Maker*, adding 'My husband absolutely loves them, thinks they're fantastic.' She concluded that, with the place packed, the music brilliant and the sun well and truly out, 'you couldn't ask for a better day.' She may not have been Welsh, and AB/CD certainly weren't, but like all those present they were granted honorary citizenship for the duration.

Next up came local punk throwbacks the Crocketts, a familiar tour support act for the Phonics who'd not been forgotten when it came to sharing some of the headliners' accumulated glory. This was a band that tended to split the audience into two distinct groups: those who'd seen them before with the headliners (pro) and those making Davey and Co's acquaintance for the first time (largely anti); certainly acceptance wasn't instant.

But when the be-shaded singer, dressed in his usual Oxfam chic and strangling his Telecaster in patented fashion, whacked out the recent single 'James Dean-esque', it seemed to serve as a rallying cry. By the climax of their act, he was emboldened enough by the audience reaction to straddle

Richard Jones

a monitor, pseudo-metal style, to deliver 'Tennessee'... and was rewarded by a near ecstatic reception.

Davey was later in understandably ebullient mood, claiming with some justification that 'the reaction was brilliant, it just went off and kicked ass. I fell over once or twice and my guitar strap broke twice, but the rest of it I liked.'

Two steps forward, then... but next came a step back as former music journalist Cliff Jones and his much-touted Gay Dad took the stage. 'I'm a Jones, I'm a Jones!' insisted the singer, desperately looking for Welsh approval... but in vain. There was more enthusiasm shown when Stuart Cable emerged from backstage to sign autographs, a healthy queue resulting. Back on stage, 'To Earth With Love', 'Dimstar' and the rest of the Dad's debut album *Leisurenoise* were delivered but the question remained: why were they here at all? 'We wouldn't be here if we didn't like the Stereophonics,' Jones sniffed when the point was put.

'Be sure to pack the sunscreen if you're going down to see the Stereophonics – because it's going to be a hot one.'

Last up before the headliners came Reef. It might not be the best spot to occupy, with the crowd potentially getting restless – but, fresh from their footballing triumph, the lads from the West Country seemed keen to repeat their earlier performance in musical terms. In a surprise move, they chose to open not with one of their many tried and tested crowd-pleasing hits but their as yet little-known forthcoming single 'New Bird'. In the end, though, it mattered not one iota. Gary Stringer, he of the gravel voice and the long curtain of hair, certainly took the gig by the scruff of the neck, being well aware from many previous festival appearances that charisma can evaporate into the open-air as quickly as *that* if you don't project.

Happily, the trouble promised by some Internet-equipped yobboes between Cardiff and Swansea football supporters wouldn't materialise – a case of all mouth and modem, perhaps – leaving the pre-gig boxing the only (strictly controlled) violence on offer. It might have been the heat of the day sapping the will to do anything but be entertained, but this was as good-natured a gathering as you'd find anywhere. Morfa's own personal weather forecast the previous evening on BBC Wales had run: 'Be sure to pack the sunscreen if you're going down to see the Stereophonics – because it's going to be a hot one.' Now the heat was about to be turned up even higher…

'I was absolutely shitting myself, I was completely in awe when we walked on stage and looked out at all those people.'

As one, the 50,000 assembled fans awaited the arrival of three men from Cwmaman. They roared as the opening chords of 'Hurry Up And Wait' crackled from the huge speakers… then up went the lights as Kelly, Richard and Stuart were revealed, the former barefoot but pacing his own length of carpet, the latter resplendent in funny, Andy Capp-style hat. As the first song's closing chords died away, Kelly greeted the audience in suitably laconic style: 'Hello, Morfa!'. The crowd's roar was, this time, even louder – and, over the next two hours, the intensity level would hardly dip. And why not? They were to enjoy 25 (count 'em) songs that rocked the derelict stadium to its creaking foundations.

The low-key, strumalong intro of 'Hurry Up And Wait' had almost seemed a self-consciously low-key choice to kick off an event which was a celebratory triumph from start to finish – one heavy-metal bible *Kerrang!* would garnish with a maximum five stars and insist proved to all-comers that 'The Stereophonics are without question the biggest band in Britain.' Kelly's post-gig reflections suggest his lack of words at the microphone might have had something to do with stage fright. 'I was absolutely shitting myself,' he'd later confess. 'I was completely in awe when we walked on stage and looked out at all those people.'

As 'The Bartender And The Thief' cranked into action, with an ever more animated Kelly happily churning out thick, churning riffs from his Gibson at breakneck speed (compared to the recorded version), the crowd's attention was suddenly diverted to the giant 25 feet high screens suspended in mid-air either side of the stage. These were happily interspersing close-ups of the band with their videos. No matter where you were, there was something to see, be it the three figures on stage or the Thailand film frolics of the vid. Meanwhile, as *Q*'s reviewer put it, '100,000 (mostly tattooed) arms punched the air – and the air stayed punched!'

'T-Shirt Suntan' made it three in a row from the just-released album – a new song to some, but one they'd first introduced to their stage repertoire as long ago as late 1996. If you'd been on stage with Kelly, you might have been surprised at how low he had his amplifiers; unlike most guitar players, he'd never been one to turn everything to maximum volume. 'I need quite a low stage level to hear my singing in the monitors,' he's explained. Likewise, his stage effects pedals have always been few and far between; a wah-wah, a Blues Driver and, most important of all, a pedal to switch between amplifiers: 'I use amps to colour the sound rather than effects pedals, because when you're singing you don't want to be messing around.'

The chart success of 'Pick A Part That's New' had everyone singing along at top volume as if they somehow sensed this was one of three songs (along with 'T-Shirt Suntan' that preceded it) that would soon appear as bonus tracks on the band's next single. If looking for a new sensation was what band and audience were seeking, then Morfa '99 was turning out to be an unrepeatable blast. Many would claim to have been there in the months to come, but those who truly were would never forget it.

Five songs into the set came the first selection from the band's debut album, now a couple of years old. The subject-matter of 'A Thousand Trees' hardly lent itself to stadium rockery (if such an expression exists), but it's just impossible not to sing along to that catchy chorus. Kelly's intro and verse sees him playing an ascending bass line on the bottom two strings – not a simple task but one, as ever, he's well up to. Richard, sporting a natty

Stuart Cable

quiff courtesy of Cwmaman's one hairdressing salon, was, as ever, quietly amused at the response. 'We don't kick in the band until about halfway through because the audience sing all of it... and that's great!'

Having delved all the way back for inspiration, the Phonics seemed to like what they'd found and followed up with a triple blast from *Word Gets Around* – 'Too Many Sandwiches', 'Not Up To You' and 'Check My Eyelids For Holes'. Kelly was still fighting back the feeling of awe as he surveyed the crowd from the large grey stage set-up which all but dwarfed the band. 'We've always admired bands like REM and U2,' he'd comment, 'but to get this big so soon is surreal. I can't believe all these people are here for *us...*'

The rendition of the rarely heard these days '...Eyelids...', was particularly spectacular, with Kelly's voice sounding more gruff and raucous than ever. The lines rasped out over the auditorium, powered by Stuart's Keith Moon-esque drums and the ever-supportive Jones bass-line. If anyone doubted the role of the rhythm section, then this was probably the number to play them. It also featured that rarity of rarities – a guitar solo from Kelly, with wah-wah a-plenty.

The crowd's ecstatic reception of the forthcoming single 'I Wouldn't Believe Your Radio' suggested it was a sterling choice to aim chartwards. This was the song Kelly 'saw in a dream' and had envisaged as a big band, Beatles-style number. Even without the assistance of the Fab Four and their Yellow Submarine, it was certainly big and brassy enough to come across to each and every person here.

The pace then came down a bit as the intensity level rose for 'She Takes Her Clothes Off', already a favourite despite not having been stripped out as a single and thus familiar to album buyers only. But no sooner had this emotional peak been achieved than the sun peeped teasingly from behind the clouds and it was time for a bit of fun. Given the venue and the occasion, the advent of the show's one cover version, 'Sunny Afternoon', in mid-set could hardly have been better timed. Did the assembled hordes realise this was nearly a quarter of a century old? Did they care? Did Welsh flags stop waving? The answer is no, no and no.

Having gone back all the way to 1966, it was time to return to November 1996 and 'More Life In A Tramp's Vest', half of the limited edition double A-sided single that had first introduced the Stereophonics to the world. Most of those who'd bought it would recall its second lease of life six months later when it became the first Phonics single to chart in the all-important Top 40. But when Kelly was lustily delivering his tale of life on a fruit'n'veg stall in provincial Wales, who the hell cared?

Though the crowd would barely have realised it, this staccato, new-wave flavoured number reminiscent of Northern Ireland's renowned Undertones from two decades earlier, was one song they were unlikely to hear too many times again. The Stereophonics, and Kelly Jones, had moved on, and their forthcoming music was likely to be light-years away from this small-town tale. 'We'll piss a few people off,' said Jones, 'but there's no way we're going to be putting out more stuff like "…Tramp's Vest". We've done our punk pop stuff now.'

The transition from Cwmaman to 'Plastic California' was almost as abrupt as the band's own rise to fame, the impact of which was still hitting Kelly, Richard and Stuart as they looked out on the assembled 50,000. The Stereophonics never took holidays, of course – they were always on the road. But that's exactly how they liked it.

On to the thought-provoking 'Is Yesterday, Tomorrow, Today?' – a great title for a song and one Kelly picked up down the social club from the son of a friend. As ever, the song was greeted with unbridled enthusiasm, flag-waving and generally word-perfect singing. It seemed amazing that the pace had yet to flag; but anyone hoping for a half-time orange would be sadly disappointed.

Having sampled *Performance And Cocktails* for a couple of songs, it was back to the first album for the lilting 'Same Size Feet' (the UK single that never was) before a switch of guitars precedes 'Traffic' – the acoustic ballad being greeted by a predictable yet still breathtaking sea of lighters. This was what *Q* magazine would call the set's 'pivotal moment... the sun, having burnt everyone lobster pink throughout the afternoon, has receded and the stars are out. The song prompts even more mutual felicity than Oasis's 'Wonderwall' at Knebworth... every last person is swaying and singing along.' It was at this moment that Nick Duerden, the magazine's

every last person is swaying and singing along.'

reviewer, also realised that 'the Stereophonics really *are* the biggest rock band in the country.'

By now Kelly's nerves had eased, and he was getting more involved with the audience, telling them where the band had been recently and what they'd been up to when they got there. It was almost as if they were all down at the club supping together at the bar, a thought which was the cue for 'Last Of The Big Time Drinkers'. But it was 'Looks Like Chaplin' that received the biggest reception, a mixed-tempo version of their first single release that 'rocked as much as everyone else's' sets put together', according to *NME*'s reviewer. Two and a half minutes dead in its recorded version, it came and went to deserved applause.

'For the whole time I was on stage I was in permanent shock, everyone there knew my name, they knew our songs... they really cared.'

Massed vocals were in evidence during the recent single 'Just Looking', followed seamlessly by 'Local Boy In The Photograph' – the last song of the set. This was one of several songs which had a lead and rhythm guitar part which couldn't be played simultaneously (unless you had three hands!). 'When you're in a three-piece,' Kelly explained later, 'there's not really enough space for all that. You've just got to concentrate on keeping everything full.' It's also a song that would take its toll on anyone's voice, and as such came dangerously late on in the set... but as with most songs today Kelly has plenty of help on the vocal front. Yet though they try their best, his rasp is particularly difficult to imitate with accuracy, even after a few pints of the local brew.

It was hard to believe that two hours and 20-odd songs had passed by in an instant, and the audience response suggested that the trio who'd vacated the stage all smiles would not be allowed to rest in backstage obscurity for *too* long.

And so it proved – though it was a solo Kelly who returned for 'As Long As We Beat The English', the song written for BBC Wales' coverage of the Five Nations Rugby. Given that each and every pause in proceedings had been greeted with massed chants of 'Waaa-les', the reception for this was always going to be ecstatic – and magnified several-fold in volume whenever footage of famous Welsh rugby victories filled the screens. 'For the whole time I was on stage I was in permanent shock,' confessed Kelly as he took a well-deserved drink. 'Everyone there knew my name, they knew our songs... they really *cared*.'

This was followed by two more solo efforts: 'Nice To Be Out', the B-side to the most recent single 'Pick A Part That's New' which would sort dedicated single-buyers from the rest while proving that the Phonics have too many great songs for their own good: how many other bands could throw away something this catchy? Then 'Billy Davey's Daughter', the sign-off track from *Word Gets Around*, performs the same service for this section of the live show and the stage is empty once again. Pandemonium...

Richard and Stuart return to the fray for the show's closing moments, which an Internet reviewer's day-after synopsis summed up perfectly for those unfortunate enough to have missed out: 'Before giving the audience the encore they wanted, the Phonics reminded them of why they should be proud to be Welsh. The enormous screens flashed images of a series of Welsh icons from over the years, sending the crowd into a Nationalistic fervour. A picture of Tom Jones sent them wild. By now, the crowd was baying for blood, and they got what they wanted, as the Stereophonics returned for the encore.

'They rocked us with a particularly loud 'Roll Up And Shine', at a time when lesser bands would be winding down. In fact, even the final song, 'I Stopped To Fill My Car Up', ended robustly and energetically. And as the final note was sung, and the final chord struck, Morfa breathed its last too...'

As the last firework fizzled, Stuart – now minus hat – was happy to give the press his considered verdict. 'That was amazing! Everything about today has been brilliant; the games, the boxing, the support bands, everything. Now I'm going to get totally *drunk*...'

chapter 2:

LIFE IN CWMAMAN

Maybe they'll give it a blue plaque some day. Aberdare General Hospital, that is, where all three Stereophonics members were born. Stuart Cable's arrival in May 1970 gives him a four-year start on to other pair. Kelly and Richard Jones, though unrelated, were born not only in the same hospital but the same month, June 1974. They'd meet for the first time in September 1978 when, as typically adventurous four year olds, they started their climb up the educational ladder at the bottom rung – nursery school.

To understand where the Stereophonics are coming from, you have to go back to Cwmaman. The small South Wales former pit village can be found off the B4275, halfway between Cardiff and Swansea in the Rhondda Valley, with one road in... and the same road out. With a population of around 1,000, it's where most of the songs on *Word Gets Around* were written, and it's a place that's very much in the trio's blood, So much so they've each bought homes there. Kelly may tell you that 'When you write good songs where you came from is unimportant,' but Phonics fans know better.

Stuart believes it's retained its character because 'you have to have a reason to go there. You can't drive through. That's why it's stayed a special place, a closed-in community.' Though the pit has long since shut, the houses were originally built for miners, the loftier ones being occupied by the colliery's bosses 'so they could look down on everybody,' says Kelly Jones. 'The power thing.'

The road of terraced houses snaking up the side of the valley ends with a highly significant full stop – the Ivy Bush public house. This was, is and always will be the lads' 'local'. Kelly credits Cwmaman as having 'a good pub culture', by which he means kids were allowed to go into licensed premises with their parents. Once upon a time he might well have been at home in front of the telly in the charge of his elder brother, but this was a curious child. Even at the age of ten he was a perceptive observer of what went on, and the Stereophonics would play some early gigs in the pub, recycling what had been heard going on into songs – even if those being written and sung about didn't always realise what was happening. Now it tends to be the opposite…

'Play football on Saturday, and in a band on a Sunday, and hopefully something works out. The band really started out through boredom.'

Kelly and Stuart lived eight doors apart on the same street, Richard's house being reached by crossing a football pitch. Opposite Kelly and Stuart's homes was Cwmaman's sole leisure facilities specifically intended for those yet to achieve legal drinking age – a public outdoor swimming pool and a park. That was inevitably where the local lads would meet up, play tapes and compare notes, and where, at the age of ten, they first conspired to form a band. 'You don't know what you want to do when you're a kid – play football on Saturday, and in a band on a Sunday, and hopefully something works out. The band really started out through boredom.'

Kelly would later write an 11-page treatment of a proposed TV script based on the self-same environment he grew up in. 'It was about a girl and everything that she was going through. The BBC gave me some money to develop it, but the band got signed. It was called *The Pool*. It's all I can remember as kids, lying on the pavements in the summer because they got really warm and when we got up we'd all be black.'

Kelly started to learn to read music but stopped soon after when the man who taught him moved up to London; he acquired his first guitar at 11. 'The old man bought it for me, a ten-quid acoustic from a catalogue,' he recalls, noting that 'the nylon strings killed my fingers. But my dad would teach me to play the song he did in the pubs; 'Pretty Woman', stuff like that.'

Stuart, who was that much older than Kelly, already had a drum kit so it was logical the younger lad should give up 'pretending to be Roy Orbison' and come out of his bedroom. A couple of loud thrashing sessions in the Jones family garage were enough to convince both that there was something there. They were an odd couple in some ways, but united in a love of classic music from the past which overcame what, to them, must then have seemed a vast age difference. 'When we did our first gig,' Kelly recalls, 'I was 12 and he must have been 16.'

The group, Zephyr (some Phonics fanatics insist it was mis-spelled Zepher), was completed by a lad blessed with the unfortunate name of Nicolas Geek, known to all and sundry as Geeky, who was a guitarist like Kelly. The bass-less trio duly returned to the garage to play enthusiastically approximate cover versions of songs by Creedence Clearwater Revival, Queen, the Eagles, Van Halen and the aforementioned Orbison.

The be-shaded 1960s star, who toured with the Beatles and was an influence on everyone from Elvis Costello to Bruce Springsteen, was at first glance an unlikely hero for a teenage garage band from sleepy south Wales. But Kelly's father, Oscar Jones, was the man to blame. He'd been the featured singer with Polydor Records signings Oscar and the Kingfishers, who had supported the American legend in the early 1970s. By that time, Orbison's star had waned somewhat and he was pounding out his hits on the 'chicken in a basket' cabaret circuit in the north of England. Oscar and 'the Big O' met at Batley Variety Club, and ever since then a 'thrilled' Jones

Senior had been a committed fan. (Orbison, who'd recently returned to the charts as a member of the Traveling Wilburys with George Harrison, Tom Petty and Bob Dylan, would sadly die from heart failure in late 1988.)

Having a dad who'd been 'in the business' at least meant Kelly didn't have to put up with constant parental moaning about getting 'a proper job'; indeed, he claims his current fame has brought the two of them closer together. He remembers being paid £5 to carry speakers to his father's pub gigs, and recounts how Oscar could have been a major star had the Hollies not took off. Even so, Kelly is still proud to state his father 'was the biggest name on the club circuit for years.'

'I absolutely love words, always have done. And I'm sticking my neck on the chopping block here, but I think Kelly's probably the best lyricist in Britain right now.'

Oscar had initially coped with the disappointment of fading stardom by taking jobs as an entertainer on cruise ships. This helped him keep his suntan topped-up, but when he realised his sons were in danger of forgetting who their dad was he opted for a job on the assembly line of a local factory, with weekend gigs squeezed in to satisfy his creative urges.

Stuart's musical education came courtesy of his brother, who'd kindly lent him the £60 necessary for the purchase of a second-hand drum kit. Stuart quickly took to Canadian progressive three-piece Rush. They were not, admittedly, the hippest name to mention in the world, but were a band that boasted a highly literate and distinctive drummer in Neil Peart, who also contributed the lyrics to the band's stop-start-stop again music. Stuart was sold. His other favourites, Deep Purple, are (like Rush) still active on the heavy-metal circuit, also with original drummer Ian Paice, whose skills with the sticks are as legendary as the band itself.

But like his main idol Peart, Stuart was that rarity – a drummer who listened to the lyrics of the songs. 'I absolutely love words,' he'd confirm in 1999, 'always have done. And I'm sticking my neck on the chopping block here, but I think Kelly's probably the best lyricist in Britain right now.'

All three Stereophonics-to-be ended up at the village school. Kelly's record as a pupil was adequate enough, though he claims only to have bonded with his metalwork teacher, Mr Merriman, 'because he used to talk about different kinds of whisky and had a big ZZ Top beard.' He certainly enjoyed English, though he won't say as much, because he'd notch up the six GCSEs which were to prove his ticket to art college.

Kelly seemed to be a winner both in the classroom and on the playing field. As previously noted, he started boxing at age ten, winning five fights before hanging up his gloves to concentrate on football – and getting so good at *that* he played for his county. Even now, he'll look to take in a football match on his occasional weekends off. Schooldays also brought Kelly into contact with Emma, his girlfriend since the age of 15 and 'my best mate as well'. They're still together today.

Stuart admits he was a dunce at school and only put in measurable effort when required to use his hands rather than engage his brain. Woodwork and art were predictable favourites, 'though I'd put in a bit more effort if I liked the teacher.' Teachers he didn't like, especially those considered 'wet liberals', stood a fair to middling chance of finding themselves locked in stockrooms!

Richard was, quite simply, a law unto himself. 'I couldn't be arsed to go to school, and got in trouble through drink a few times. You know, someone picks on you, you have a fight and end up in the cells.' Kelly remembers his pal bunking off all day to pour his money down the throats of the one-armed bandits. 'I think he pinched the odd car with a few other boys, but nothing serious.' Once he left school, needless to say at the first available opportunity, Richard scraped a living as a coalman, an electrician, a plumber and a labourer.

Wanting to look older so that he'd be served in the local pub, he rashly had his name tattooed on his neck. There'd be eight more permanent decorations, gathered between the ages of 15 and 17 and all of which, he now admits, he regrets. A hairy skull adorns his chest, while a shining sun surrounds his belly button and his arms are each heavily illustrated. The neck tattoo, though, remains the most obvious and is now a candidate for removal by the supposedly painless laser beam method.

The earliest exploits of our threesome often bordered on the mildly illegal – a fact they're happy to admit. Kelly and Stuart both had brushes with the law when they attempted, separately, to nick heavy metal tapes from Woolworths. Kelly was dissuaded from ever doing it again when his mum took him shopping for new jeans 'and I had this *Deep Purple In Rock* tape down my pants.' Stuart was less lucky, but took consolation from the fact that a wasp stung the store detective who collared him. 'It was worth pinching the tape to see that happen!' he chortles.

Richard, who claims 'I weren't a big thief,' nevertheless admits to being involved in a car theft in which he attempted to stay out of trouble by pretending to be asleep in the back of said vehicle! Stuart, for his part, was arrested one fireworks night for siphoning petrol out of a car to light the bonfire. 'The guy came out and chased us up the mountain. Then the police came round my house a few days later but my mother wouldn't let them take me away for fingerprints. She stood her ground.' If the redoubtable Mabel Cable hadn't been enough, the prospect of Stuart's brother's dog – 'a real hard nut' – might also have dissuaded them from further action. Compared with that, Kelly's nearest brush with the law – being moved on when he decided, in an inebriated state, to do press-ups outside a pub – sounds pretty dull stuff.

The Jones boy did, however, take his drinking seriously, and recalls one fateful night at the pub when he was around 17. The tipple of choice on this occasion was wine and lemonade mixed together, but his pal behind the bar wasn't diluting Kelly's glass like the others. The evening climaxed with a spectacular rendition of Otis Redding's 'Dock Of The Bay' on the resident karaoke, but things could have turned nasty when Kelly went home and was sick in his sleep. Fortunately, his mother had turned him over; if she hadn't, he probably could have died. Which is just as well, because today he cites his greatest fear as 'dying before I finish doing everything I want to do.'

Zephyr had blown itself out, as first bands tend to, Kelly and Geeky having had the ultimate unwinnable squabble as to whose guitar should be

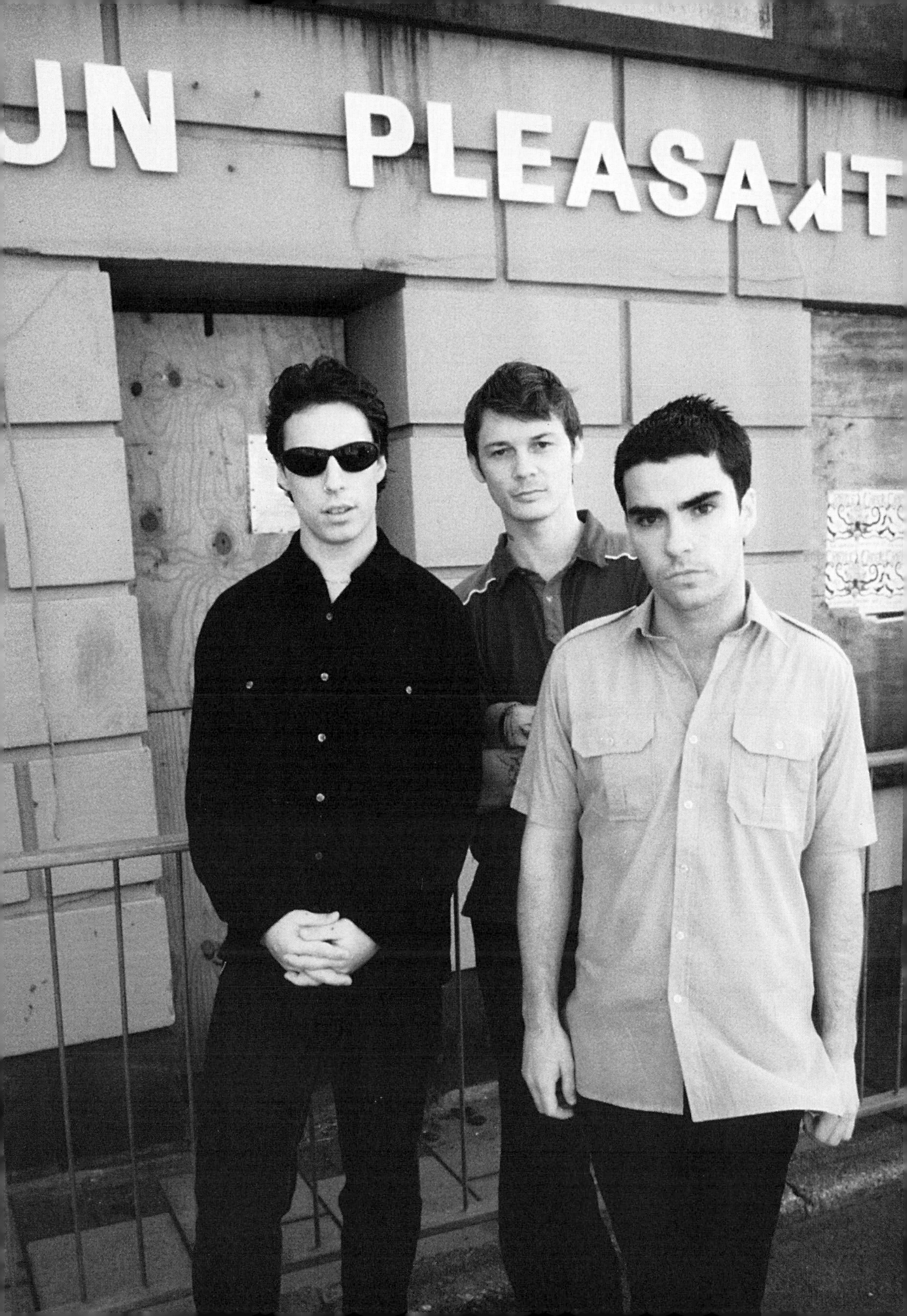
UN PLEASANT

the louder. Presumably neither was keen to swop six strings for four. Both Stuart and Kelly joined other bands; King Catwalk and Silent Runner respectively. The pair wouldn't speak for over a year, as they pursued their separate paths. Silent Runner's musical fare was American adult-oriented rock of the ilk of Bob Seger, Journey, Blue Oyster Cult and REO Speedwagon, while Stuart's band, by all accounts (including his own) were glam throwbacks who demanded he wear lipstick on stage! Neither could have been completely satisfied with what they were doing, because in 1989 Kelly approached his former musical partner in the bar of the Ivy Bush and proposed they rekindle their relationship. The result was Tragic Love Company.

The name of the band was an amalgamation of acts they admired – the Tragically Hip, Mother Love Bone and Bad Company. While the former were (and are) politically correct Canadian guitar-rockers and Mother Love Bone a Seattle group containing two future members of Pearl Jam, the last-named stand out like a sore thumb. Cock-rock kings of the pre-punk 1970s who emigrated to tax exile land and made a million in the States. But the real connection is Paul Rodgers, the singer who'd first found fame with Free, of 'All Right Now' fame. It's a heritage they shared with Reef, whose name happens to be a close relation.

Every band demands commitment from its members, and Tragic Love Company were no exception. There have been many legendary early departures from bands, the first probably Pete Best's departure from the Beatles which left him with the title of 'the nearly man of rock'. The name of the new band's bassist doesn't seem to have entered the public domain, but it's certain he must now feel he's the 'Pete Best of the Valleys'. Because when he went on holiday, 14 year old Richard Jones stepped into his still-warm shoes... and stayed there.

As previously recounted, Richard had long been a non-musical pal of the other pair, so no introduction was necessary. 'The three of us have always done everything together,' Stuart explains. 'If you saw one of us, the other two were there.' Kelly, still the smallest of the trio at five foot five in his stockinged feet, recalls how one summer he cut his leg and couldn't walk. 'Richard used to pick me up and dip my head in the swimming pool to keep me cool. I took him on holiday to Barry Island to thank him.'

For the young Richard, picking up the bass guitar (rather than picking up Kelly) was a matter of spending what he earned during two years 'on the milk' delivering Cwmaman's early-morning pinta; he went out and bought a fretless instrument, quite an adventurous choice for a beginner. His father bought him a Fender amplifier, but he grew tired of having to hit the correct intonation and shifted to guitar after a couple of years. Fortunately, he'd switched back to his first love – fretted, this time, for maximum effect – when Kelly and Stuart lost the services of that holidaying four-stringer. They only asked him to play for two weeks...

Richard's style cemented another Free/Bad Company link by echoing the work of Andy Fraser. He supplied a lot of Free's lead lines, a habit Richard Jones has been happy to aspire to, following the absence of fret-melting guitar licks from Kelly. As for his stage role, he explained to *Kerrang!* that his aim was to be '...just like any other bass player – hanging back and looking cool.'

The image certainly struck a chord with Stuart, who recalls the new recruit turning up to audition for them with hair down to his waistband. 'He looked fucking ice cool. He slung this bass round his hip and just started hitting the four strings... I don't think he had a *clue* what he was doing. But me and Kelly looked at each other and went "Now that's what I call a fucking *bass player*".' For the record, the trio cut their teeth that day on two Lenny Kravitz songs they found they all knew: 'Mr Cab Driver' and 'Let Love Rule'; both are from his first album, which dates the first rehearsal at perhaps early 1990.

The kind of gigs the trio were playing saw them encounter every type of audience imaginable. The very first show, booked by Kelly's dad on behalf of the Cwmaman Social and Working Men's Club, was typical in teaching them that they were on stage not to please themselves but to entertain with a capital E. 'If you didn't, you got thrown off stage.' Early gigs saw people with their feet up on the stage reading a newspaper, 'not giving a fuck.'

Stuart agrees, explaining that, if ten people clap at a Stereophonics gig, and they've done their best, then that's good enough for them; bands who've only ever played in London to the music business, they all feel, have missed out. The key is not to try to impress but 'enjoy it and entertain people.'

The one thing the band drew the line at doing was dressing up in anything too out of the ordinary. Regulation gear was check shirt, denim jacket and, if it was a good week, leather trousers. 'It was sacrilege in Cwmaman not to wear a check shirt because everyone was into Neil Young. But to be *really* cool, you weren't allowed to wash for three weeks!'

The trio's musical endeavours were hardly making them a living; far from it. Stuart admits he was signing on the dole while looking round for casual work on building sites for £20 a day for mixing cement or carrying bricks. Maybe in retrospect this fetching and carrying helped him develop the stamina to play two hour plus sets each night of a long tour... and you

can take it the pay's improved! July 1990 saw Kelly quit school with six GCSEs. Art college followed, his paltry grant augmented by work as a £16 a day 'Saturday boy' (plus Fridays and summer holidays) on a fruit and vegetable stall in nearby Aberdare market.

The BBC Radio 1 documentary team tracked down his boss there, Phil Rees, in 1999, who declared his former employee 'good with the public'. He also revealed the other Saturday boy, known as Mac the Knife, was 'so quiet there's more life in a tramp's vest'... a phrase that would become more than familiar to Phonics fans later. Kelly would gain inspiration from his surroundings and the people he met, scribbling scraps of lyrics on the stall's brown paper bags. 'I'd pick up a bag to give to a customer,' Phil Rees recalled gleefully, 'and there's be a song on the back of it!' That's got to be worth money nowadays...

Kelly, who'd work there until the Stereophonics were signed up, recalls this market experience as 'a good crack, working outside in the summer... (watching all the) characters coming in and out.' Old ladies would come to the stall just to be entertained by the 16 year old juggling sprouts and honing his entertainment skills. The market trader's traditional cries must have toughened up his voice, too.

Certainly he enjoyed his stint of interaction with the public more than art college, where 'people go 'cos they don't know what to do. The majority of people there are dickheads because they're there to get money to buy Minis and guitars, things like that. That's not really what it's about.' (On the other hand, the likes of Ron Wood, Pete Townshend and Freddie Mercury all emerged from that breeding ground.) Kelly's course had introduced him to animation, but it drove him mad. 'How anyone can do that for a living and not go absolutely bonkers is beyond me. 24 drawings for one second of footage? Nah – let's go down the pub.'

Tragic Love Company's terminally unoriginal name finally bit the dust in July 1996, and their singer, for one, wasn't unhappy about that. He once phoned a venue to ask for a gig only to be told 'Sorry... did you say you were Mr Kelly from Charter Oil Company?'

The catalyst for change had been a forthcoming gig at a converted theatre, the Aberdare Coliseum, where they'd be supporting an up-and-coming band called Catatonia and playing to a bigger crowd than usual.

The headliners' manager loved the demo tape they'd sent, but hated the name. Could they call themselves something else? Of *course* they could!

The derivation of the name Stereophonics has already gone down in rock legend alongside Buffalo Springfield taking their distinctive handle from a sign on the side of a steamroller. But just like many rock myths it exists in several different forms. The word 'Stereophonic', so the official version reads, was spied on an old-fashioned gramophone record player owned by Stuart's grandmother, and certainly whoever came up with it did so just a matter of days before the big gig. Nowadays, of course, it has its own typeface and has become a fully-fledged logo.

'I was forced into singing by Stuart, who used to put matches under my fingernails to make me sing Led Zeppelin songs in the right key.'

Musically speaking, the band's set now included Kelly's first songs mixed in with cover versions; not unnaturally, these originals took on some of their flavour from the other material. And having elder brothers and sisters proved as rewarding in the musical sense as it could be annoying in other aspects of family life. Richard, for instance, grew up on a diet of everything from progressive (Genesis), reggae (Bob Marley) and punk (the Clash). 'Things become influences without you knowing,' he comments today.

The new band finally gave Kelly the chance to be fulfilled as a songwriter; that had always been his major goal in music, since he hadn't really considered himself much of a guitarist or a singer. He still doesn't... 'I can't play a fucking guitar solo to save my life,' he happily admitted to *Making Music* magazine after the first album was released. 'That's why I kill my throat so much. I was forced into singing by Stuart, who used to put matches under my fingernails to make me sing Led Zeppelin songs in the right key. That's why I sound like I smoke 200 Regals a day – even though I don't smoke.'

Musical inspiration for the young Kelly Jones came mainly from his father's record collection and, aside from Roy Orbison, often tended towards soul; his favourites were Otis Redding and Sam Cooke, both long dead. There was a jazz influence, too; the band would later cut a B-side bonus version of 'Summertime', the *Porgy And Bess* showstopper made famous by Billie Holiday. His brother Kevin, meanwhile, is now the Stereophonics' road manager but deserves praise for introducing the lad to AC/DC.

The fact the younger Jones' main instrument today is a cherry-red, double-cutaway Gibson SG is in deference to the Aussie metallers' axeman-in-chief Angus Young. For non-followers, the diminutive Angus also dressed as a schoolboy and played solos with his SG on top of bandmates' shoulders. 'They were a meat and potatoes band,' confesses Kelly, 'but they were one of the tightest you could watch.' Now you understand why Morfa kicked off with a tribute act…

Also a big presence in the trio's collective consciousness was Creedence Clearwater Revival. Like the Stereophonics, their creative focus was a singer, guitarist and songwriter – John Fogerty, a particular hero to Richard. On the day he wrote 'Proud Mary' (a Transatlantic Top 10 hit in 1969) he wrote four other songs. Kelly agrees with the bass-player's assessment, calling Fogerty's output 'constant, prolific writing... every song a classic.'

The embryonic Phonics/Tragic Love Company been encouraged to play their own stuff by the then landlord of the Ivy Bush, Graham Davies. Kelly would ask him to listen critically to what he was writing, and took the points he made to heart. One of the demo tapes they made was also to win praise in *Melody Maker*'s review column hosted by a certain Holly Hernandez. The lady in question, whose visage adorned the page topped with a set of devil's horns, specialised in handing out jaw-droppingly uncomplimentary reviews of unsigned bands' offerings. Amazingly, she liked what she heard... and an allegiance with the paper sprang up that continues to this day.

Stuart remembers regretting the tape had ever been sent, 'because she used to rip into everybody. And then in the space of 18 months or so we were on the cover of the paper we'd been buying every week.' With the band taping themselves regularly, there's some confusion as to what actually popped through Holly's postbox. Kelly, who ought to know, believes it contained a full band version of 'Billy Davey's Daughter'.

There would be a later, legendary demo containing three compositions – 'Looks Like Chaplin', 'More Life In A Tramp's Vest' and 'A Thousand Trees', all songs strong enough to be later released as singles. Little wonder it won them the Catatonia gig. 'A Thousand Trees' from the three-song demo was aired by Radio 1's Steve Lamacq on his 'Session Unsigned' portion of the *Evening Session* show, and has often been requested to be replayed. The duo who helped them produce this studio-quality tape were Marshall Bird and Steve Bush, an unknown pairing who worked at a recording studio in north-west London.

Bird and Bush would reap the rewards when the Stereophonics elected to keep them as their production team been after they were signed. It was a typically loyal decision, and sensible too in that they'd discovered early on how best to get their sound onto tape – why alter things by enlisting a big-name producer who might want to change them?

The initial connection was made back in March 1996, when the band had been supporting a Sunderland outfit called Smalltown Heroes (ironically, a highly appropriate name for the Stereophonics!) at London's small but media-haunted Borderline Club just off the Charing Cross Road. This had been one of the band's first ventures to London (as Tragic Love Company) and predated even their hook-up with management. Bird and Bush had been in the audience, liked what they heard and approached the band afterwards. It was a helping hand they'd appreciate.

Playing London dates was a real shock to the system; Richard and Stuart would take the afternoon off, drive up to the gig, then speed home through the night to resume everyday life with an hour or two's sleep between them if they were really lucky. The worst part was that the tape player in Stuart's van wouldn't work unless someone put their finger on the button... and kept it pressed! You can take it there was no rush to sit in the front seat; in fact spending time huddled up in the back with the amps and instruments become a positive pleasure! Another recurring problem was finding the £1 toll demanded by the Severn Bridge linking England with Wales. The solution? 'Throw a few pence into the coin drop and drive like fuck!'

While Richard paid the bills with a spot of plumbing, Kelly studied and Stuart delivered school meals around the area. The trio spent their evenings serving up classic rock to the working men's clubs of the locality. It was an apprenticeship that would often seem unrewarding – but ultimately stood them in good stead.

As for what they played, this varied from classic metal to indie-rock and back again. Aerosmith and the Black Crowes were particular favourites and – far into the future – it would give the Phonics great pleasure to share the Wembley Stadium stage with these revered rockers. It was, perhaps, an indication of ebbing and flowing musical trends that those two names were considerably trendier to drop in 1999 than when the group first started covering their songs.

When it first came to coming up with original material, it had soon become clear that Kelly had the songwriting chops they'd need to graduate from the covers class. And that was hardly surprising; he'd moved on from combining art college and the market stall to begin a six-week scriptwriting course at Cardiff's Chapel Arts Centre. It's something he clearly enjoyed, and plans to take up again 'when we get our year off.' His great heroes included John Sullivan, creator of Del Boy, Rodders and the rest of the *Only Fools And Horses* gang. 'Fifteen years of stories, every one different. Now *that's* class writing. Now it was a question of turning the scripts in his head into three minute hits.

There would be no complaints from the rhythm section; neither Stuart nor Richard were frustrated songwriters, and understood full well that their role was to be a supporting one. 'We know the guitar and the lyrics provide the aspect of the song so we tend to use them and just support them, not try to show off,' explained Richard.

The three-piece format had survived several attempts to augment it, including Simon Collier, who'd played with them for a while before settling down to his later (and current) role as Kelly's guitar tech. Then, bizarrely, there was another Richard Jones, who'd played guitar rather than bass like his namesake. Maybe one Richard Jones in a band was enough! Finally came a guy called Glen Hyde who hailed from Merthyr. He was a good guitarist and could well have been with the band now. The guy just stopped coming to their Thursday evening practices five months before the band got picked up – perhaps the travelling got too much – but, happily, didn't hold a grudge. 'We still see him about, and he loves the fact we're doing well.'

Richard Jones the bassist is certainly happy they stuck with their trio format, feeling that adding to the line-up 'just didn't work. There were too many different styles coming into the band. The three of us work really well as a unit, and whenever a fourth member came in it was like putting Keith Moon into Take That.'

They'd sent their tapes to the record companies in London, and just as regularly they'd be returned, often unlistened-to. The gimmicks the boys employed to catch the attention of the unheeding labels are worth a book in themselves: unusual mailing containers employed included crisp boxes and a foil carton from a Chinese takeaway, while exotic accompaniments included carrot cake and even a pair of shoes. Little wonder, as Kelly put it, 'The lady at the post office thought I was a fucking idiot!' Certainly, as Stuart observes, 'a fiver of your dole money to post a package isn't cheap.'

But belief in their songs didn't wane and, to the evident disapproval of the working men's club crowds, the familiar cover versions were gradually augmented, then supplanted, by altogether more challenging fare. Though there'd never be an official leader of the group, it also focused attention on Kelly, whose 'doe eyes' and 'chiselled features' (to quote one gushing early review) would become the face of the Stereophonics. It was to be hoped that, if he was to be the Welsh Paul Weller, his colleagues would not end up the embittered Foxton and Buckler of the Valleys…

The Jam were managed by Paul's dad – but though Oscar Jones knew the showbiz ropes to some extent, the man to whose guidance the Stereophonics wisely entrusted themselves was an outsider, John Brand. He had been at the Catatonia gig at Aberdare, and the support act caught his ear. 'I remember sitting in the balcony and being extremely impressed,' he told Radio 1, adding that Kelly had found an old fur coat backstage and, on a whim, decided to wear it. The effect certainly reached the expensive seats, an awestruck Brand considering him 'the complete rock star; the songs were brilliant and really powerful.'

It was a miracle anyone had turned up to the gig, given that it coincided with a Five Nations rugby match. But as it transpired both band

and manager would remember 2 March 1996 as the day that changed their lives. Brand was then managing a female-fronted indie band called Pooka, and had come to Wales for a music seminar. His former charges had included teen act Bros, a pair of photogenic blond brothers who'd topped the charts regularly in the late 1980s. Being male and guitar-based, the Stereophonics presumably fell somewhere in the gulf between the two…

A meeting was arranged at a service station on the M4 motorway – equidistant between London and Cwmaman – a few days after the show, where the band presented him with a tape containing 'Looks Look Chaplin', 'She Takes Her Clothes Off' and 'More Life In A Tramp's Vest', plus a thick sheaf of Kelly's lyrics. In turn, they were promised a record deal within six months; music to any hopeful outfit's ears. John Brand also insisted that he 'would bring London to them' and not make them relocate to the big city where everything supposedly happened but so many promising bands came to grief.

He kept his promise: in Kelly's words, 'From nobody wanting to sign us, *everybody* wanted to sign us.' Things had certainly changed in double-quick time for the three local lads in the photograph... they were now very much in the fame frame. A Newport showcase at the Filling Station (a live music venue, not another motorway service area!) saw no fewer than 35 record-company honchos on the guest list to swell the throng... but what happened afterwards was later dubbed by Kelly 'The strangest night *ever*...

'We drove back home in Stuart's camper van, and it started to break down in the middle of nowhere! We were all sitting in the front seat thinking, "For fuck's sake, we've got every record company in Britain wanting to sign us, and here we are driving home in a poxy van with a flat battery!"' Though they were convinced the ailing vehicle was going to stop at any moment, it crawled back to Cwmaman to conveniently give up the ghost and rattle its last just outside Stuart's front door.

'For fuck's sake, we've got every record company in Britain wanting to sign us, and here we are driving home in a poxy van with a flat battery!'

The Stereophonics' earliest brushes with the music business would have made an entertaining film in their own right. One unforgettable experience came when they were invited to a London launch party for Kula Shaker, held by Columbia Records. They saw more stars that night than astronomer Patrick Moore's telescope, among whom were Jarvis Cocker ('totally down to earth, a really nice bloke') and Robbie Williams. They found they couldn't buy a beer with cash (credit cards only at the bar), and after making their displeasure known were ejected. Legend has it the man with his hand on their collective collar was a record-company executive, miffed when they let slip the fact they weren't going to sign to his label after all!

Undaunted, they moved on, next stop being the trendy Groucho Club. There they rubbed shoulders with Bob Mortimer and Stephen Fry, as well as falling down some stairs (no pain was felt). The next day they hit the town with £500 cash in each member's pocket and blew the lot on Oxford Street before returning home tired but happy.

When the trio went out on their first tour, supporting AC Acoustics, the whole village (or so it seemed) turned out onto the street to wave them off. 'It was like going off to war,' Stuart recalls. Cwmaman was 'a brilliant place to live, a good close community', and they have always resisted any invitation to badmouth their background. 'When we started doing interviews, everybody thought we wanted to escape because we didn't like where we come from. That's completely not the case. I've got to be honest, job opportunities are crap, there's not a lot there. But for peace of mind, knowing you're safe in your house, having a good time, and a close community environment where everybody talks to you, it's brilliant.'

It was ironic that they should have been spotted on their own patch. As previously recounted, the Stereophonics had ventured to the capital a number of times to play so-called 'showcase' gigs at which record labels were supposedly present in numbers. Nothing had ever come of it, and the band had slunk back across the border, collective tail between their legs, wondering why they'd scrimped, saved and sold veg to pay for the petrol money.

'We were never frightened by other bands,' reasoned Kelly, pointing out that their companions on the bill were often serving up what they thought the record companies would want. 'They only play for A&R people, whereas when you're up here and don't know what you're supposed to be doing, you do your own thing.' That way, he concluded, 'when they do find you, at least you're half original.'

But no-one can afford to look backwards. Just as the title of their first album *Word Gets Around* successfully evoked the idea of gossip spreading through a neighbourhood, so *Performance And Cocktails* – taken from a flyer for a New York club called Shine they picked up on their first or second Big Apple gig – would show how expanding their geographical horizons had an effect on their music. That was all in the future, though: first they had to find a record label.

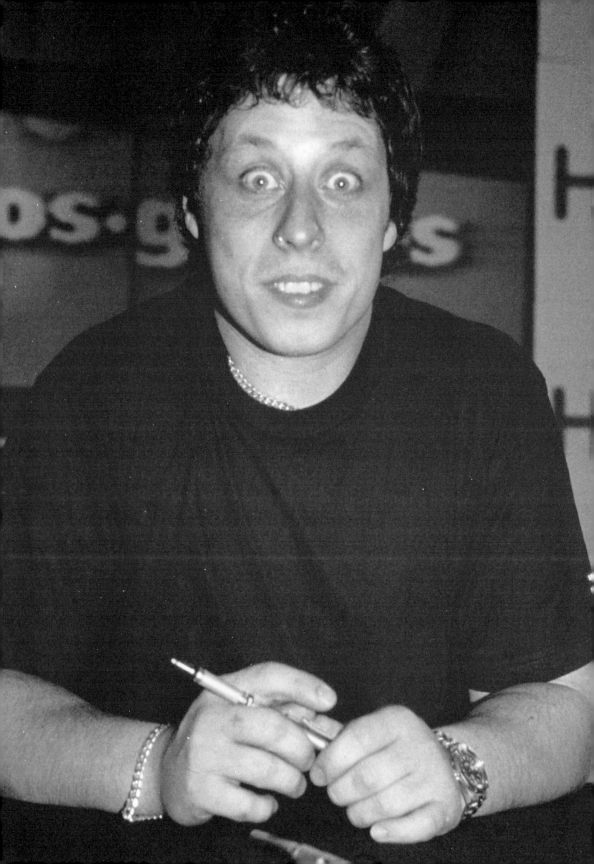

chapter 3:

SECOND-TIME VIRGINS

The Sex Pistols and the Rolling Stones... two great British bands who were spotted and signed by Richard Branson. Admittedly, Jagger and company had been at the top of the tree when the bearded wonder made his move, but it was an audacious bid against the big multinational record companies and one that shot his Virgin label into the premier league. It let him bid successfully for the likes of Janet Jackson.

Sadly the Virgin label itself was swallowed up by EMI, one of those self-same conglomerates and, ironically, the company that had offed the Pistols due to their anti-social behaviour (Sid Vicious crapping in a wastepaper basket). They'd also been former employees to the Stones.

As soon as he could, Branson decided to get back into the record business. The name of the new label, V2 was both low-key and self-explanatory. Quite how you could be a virgin for a second time was open to debate, but he wasn't short of recruits to help him get the new venture off the ground. A number of music-biz movers and shakers with impressive track records were soon knocking at his door, and the next step after assembling a dream team was to find the dream band to form the cornerstone of the V2 roster. Enter the Stereophonics...

'V2 seemed to have all the old 1970s ethics that we liked,' Kelly explained, adding that it hadn't been a matter of money – Sony had supposedly offered the most cash. V2's advance, rumoured to be £265,000 was accompanied by a masterplan that was stunning in its simplicity. 'They suggested making an album every year and touring constantly, which is how Led Zeppelin did it. They weren't going to market us through the process, they wanted to send us out and build a fan base.' Needless to say, the tactic worked like clockwork.

They'd been spotted by former music journalist Ronnie Gurr on his very first day as a V2 employee. He received a tip-off by an acquaintance living in Newport that there was a local band there about to make good. 'I went to see them without having heard them first, and I was knocked out. They were already the finished article.' Seems this pal in Newport had been spreading the word far and wide, because numerous other A&R men had wended their way westwards and were similarly impressed.

The label's general manager David Steele now recalls the demo tape they'd received as being 'absolutely fantastic – one of the best I'd heard in a long time. We were all excited. There were only three of us here then.' He pinpointed 'A Thousand Trees' as the standout. Ecstatic at spotting these diamonds in the rough, shrewd Scotsman Ronnie Gurr realised the band would have to show real faith in him just as he had in them – his label didn't even have their own offices yet, and a distribution deal was still on the horizon. But he was 'always confident that the potential would sway them.'

'We signed with V2,' explained Stuart, 'because we knew that, as their first band, we'd have to be a priority. We joined the label before many of the people who work there now. When we go in and see people we don't know, we just ask "who are *you*?"' Kelly later said of Richard Branson that 'he owns an airline, but he doesn't fly the planes'; however, he revealed to readers of music business paper *Music Week* that Branson had, in fact, involved himself personally in the signing. 'He phoned us from his island, Necker. He wasn't pushy, he just wanted to know whether we'd made up our minds.' He also said that if they did sign to his label, 'we'll be 200 per cent behind you'.

'It takes the pressure off the three of us having really good friends from back home around...

It did the trick; they signed, and Ronnie Gurr was ecstatic. He reckoned they'd be 'spoilt for choice when it comes to picking singles. Kelly writes great songs, little short stories about life.' And when the young managers association IMF voted the band 'Best New Signing of 1996', it seemed clear he was far from the only one impressed. The plan was for the Stereophonics to record their first album in-between gigs, and they made a declaration of intent by spending their first royalty advance on a tour bus. This took them to several different destinations during the last half of 1996, (including Cambridge where a paltry 30 people turned up at the Boat Race venue to see them) and Cardiff University, just down the road, where local fans swelled the attendance to 400 – the most people they'd played to as yet.

V2's Gurr approved of this continuing street-level approach which gave them the chance to 'play around with their set and see what works without a lot of pressure.' Concerts at the moment were running at around ten songs, and, though the odd audience member occasionally complained at the quantity, the quality was already beyond question. Just to keep their feet on the ground, Kelly was still receiving rejection letters in his mail. 'I had a letter back from PolyGram saying they didn't like our demo tape, and we'd already signed the fucking deal!'

The first single was recorded at Battery Studios in north London with Bird and Bush 'behind the glass'. The fact that V2 weren't insisting on big-name producers was a plus, and the song selected to make their first mark on the music map was 'Looks Like Chaplin', released on 11 November as a double A-side, limited edition with the splendidly titled market tale 'More Life In A Tramp's Vest'.

As well as being the record company name, V2 was also the designation of a German rocket weapon in World War II. Would the label's first single fly like a bird or display all the aerodynamic properties of a stone and bomb ignominiously? Only time would tell...

if we don't want to talk to each other we can talk to the crew.'

The band ventured to London for the first time as the Stereophonics, and Radio 1 were already interested enough to put them on air for an interview. Richard, asked about his hopes for the coming year of 1997, said: 'Hopefully get as many people to see us as possible and as many to hear us as possible, to get to know us, to get to like us and enjoy what we do.' He'd soon get his wish as, within a matter of weeks, they'd moved up the rock ladder from supporting north-east riot girls Kenickie to snag support spots with big-shots the Manic Street Preachers and the Who. All this in the month of December '96.

Kelly recalls having to buy longer guitar leads to play the big stages, then getting out his short one as they returned to venues like Reading's Alley Cat. It blew his mind to play at Earl's Court with the Who, a venue so big you had to leave the dressing room (itself as big as some venues they'd played) fully five minutes before you were due on stage! Supporting the Manics at London's Brixton Academy meant playing to 4,000 people – a considerable increase on the small but dedicated huddle they'd played to in a pub in Camden Town just weeks before.

Sharing a stage with the Who (at Pete Townshend's personal request, apparently) was an eye-opener for the boys in more ways than one. For the legends were, it seems, a band in name only these days. Three and a half long decades of co-existing had, it seemed, left them barely standing the sight of each other. 'We saw them all arrive in separate cars and leave in separate cars,' an unimpressed Kelly told *Q* magazine.

That wasn't at all the way it was with the Stereophonics, whose road crew were led by Kevin Jones and included nine more old pals from Cwmaman, right down to Julian, the driver who sells the T-shirts. It was almost an attempt to take a bit of Cwmaman around the world with them, like the man in the McDonald's ads who wears a piece of carpet on each foot. Stuart would describe the entourage as 'like a rugby trip that goes on for years instead of weekends,' and would typify the Stereophonic 'all for one and one for all' mentality. 'It takes the pressure off the three of us having really good friends from back home around,' explains Richard Jones. 'If we don't want to talk to each other we can talk to the crew.'

But there'd been enough talk – with 1997 fast approaching, it was time for action…

chapter 4:

LOCAL BOYS MAKE GOOD

Though December found the Stereophonics playing to their biggest audience ever – bigger, in fact, than most bands can ever dream about – as support to 1960s legends the Who, it was working with the Manic Street Preachers that gave Stuart his biggest thrill – particularly when their singer, James Lee Bradfield, looked on from the wings. 'You get a little bit nervous when James is watching you,' the usually carefree drummer admitted, 'but he's a really nice guy. He's quite shy. But once he gets to know you he's very nice. He always gives us messages to say hello and we give some back. Nice people, obviously nice people – they're Welsh, so…'

But the final day of the year that had brought so much saw them entertaining a different bunch of Celts entirely: 250,000 rabid Scots at a Hogmanay Festival in Edinburgh. Three months later came the second single, 'Local Boy In The Photograph', which reached Number 51 in the UK charts – and, emboldened by this sign of public acceptance, the band headed off on their first headlining tour of the UK, including a St David's Day special at the Coal Exchange, Cardiff, on 1 March.

The rest of the month would see them supporting Skunk Anansie on their UK tour. Both bands took to each other with enthusiasm, and Skunk's guitarist Ace was especially impressed with an unusually laid-back little song called 'Traffic' which, he predicted, would one day be a massive hit single. Give that man a medal…

Not all the gigs that year turned out to be great ones. Two in particular the Phonics might like to forget happened in Brighton and London. The first, at the so-called Essential Festival, came after driving down from Newcastle, where they'd played a midnight show, only to find they were due back on stage, warming up an exceptionally sparse crowd, at one o'clock in the afternoon – a very un-rock'n'roll hour indeed! Understandably, Kelly's voice protested under the strain, and the boys agreed as one to end their set after just three songs. The message was for the powers-that-be to plan their touring schedule a bit more proficiently, and it seemed to hit home.

'We don't know any Welsh bands and we don't sound like any of them. We don't even speak Welsh.'

Their worst gig in the capital was for a good cause – Radio 1 DJ John Peel, whose late-August birthday was being celebrated at London's Institute of Contemporary Arts. The Stereophonics had been happy to be invited to open proceedings – but since the radio broadcast started at eight o'clock and the doors opened half an hour later, they found themselves playing to an empty venue. What was worse, it was in mid-tour, and a gig to real, paying punters had been cancelled to fit in the engagement. 'The only people there,' fumed Kelly, 'were our crew and (DJ) Steve Lamacq, looking really embarrassed… a *nightmare.*'

The press were beginning to take notice now a couple of singles had escaped, but lazy journalists started putting them in a 'new wave of Welsh rock' bag with the Manics, Catatonia, Super Furry Animals and 60ft Dolls. Kelly begged to differ. 'We like the Kinks, AC/DC, Radiohead. We don't know any Welsh bands and we don't sound like any of them. We don't even speak Welsh.' He also, tongue-in-cheek, suggested that since the Manics 'were four and they lost one (member), it's more like *they're* copying *us…*'

Richard was mildly incensed that 'People tend to think that Wales is a big city, where all the bands know each other. But Wales is a big country, it's about 500 square miles big, and the bands come from different areas. The bands never come together – we didn't know the Manics until we did the gigs with them, we had never met them before. And it's the same with the Super Furries, Gorky's, Catatonia and all the other bands. The media tend to think that Wales is the next special place.'

Stuart agreed. 'There are three million people living in our country, it's not very big but it's also not very small. In the end of the day it's a country and not a city.' For Stuart, going to London would mean more than a loss of identity. 'You'd just go to celebrity parties and never write any songs.' Kelly chimes in: 'We don't go to celebrity parties and shag supermodels.' Perhaps the reason the Stereophonics have fought shy of being associated with any Welsh musical movement is because any so-called scene will eventually end.

Six months on from its tentative release as a double A-side with 'Looks Like Chaplin', 'More Life In A Tramp's Vest' belied its title by winning a full (re-)release on 19 May. Available in two CD versions and seven-inch limited edition vinyl, it was combined with two brand-new tracks, 'Raymond's Shop' and 'Poppy Day' for one CD, while the second, a live release, featured concert performances of 'Looks Like Chaplin', 'Too Many Sandwiches' and 'Last Of The Big Time Drinkers' recorded for Radio 1 barely two months earlier. The package entered the charts at Number 33 but daytime airplay was disappointing – a perennial complaint from new bands. Despite their appearance on TV's Later With Jools Holland', no sooner had 'More Life…' shown up in the listing than it crashed back out again.

But there was considerable consolation to be had the same month when the band were invited to play at the Hillsborough Benefit Concert in Liverpool. They were among the least well-known of a star-studded line-up that included home-town heroes Space and the Lightning Seeds, the Manics, the Beautiful South and Dodgy. The cause was to raise funds and awareness for the families of the 96 people who died at Sheffield Wednesday's football ground on FA Cup Semi-Final day in 1989.

Richard considered the band 'privileged' to play in such company, while for Stuart, a self confessed Liverpool fan, the chance to play at the Anfield stadium was 'the best part.' The only thing to mar a tremendous early afternoon set was the fact it was raining and Kelly suffered a succession of electric shocks.

The last six months had taken their toll on the band, and June dates were postponed in favour of a well-deserved break. Kelly busied himself writing songs back home in Cwmaman for the band's next album which, although the first hadn't hit the racks yet, was already being scheduled for recording in the coming November and release in the spring of 1999. Talk about forward planning! Rather more pressing engagements for the summer included a tour of Scandinavia, where they'd play the Swedish Hultsfred Festival in July, and The Belfort Festival in France, as well as T In The Park, the One for the People Festival at Stockton and the Phoenix Festival.

They'd return to their roots in August by playing Cardiff's annual free festival The Big Weekend, its stage situated in the very heart of the capital on the lawn in front of the Museum and City Hall. The previous year's headliners had been the highly rated Super Furry Animals, so it was clear the Phonics were on the way up. A highlight of their performance was 'A Thousand Trees', the band's next single released in mid-August. A song that built inexorably from softly-strummed beginnings to an epic chorus, it was already receiving more countrywide airplay than its predecessors, having made the B-List of the Radio 1 playlist. Virgin Radio 1215 were also enthusiastic supporters.

As well as the new track 'Carrot Cake And Wine', which would soon become something of a stage staple, the first CD included a live version of 'A Thousand Trees' recorded for Radio 1. The bonus CD to accompany the release saw the Stereophonics go 'unplugged' when performing 'A Thousand Trees' and 'Looks Like Chaplin' in acoustic fashion alongside a new song, 'Home To Me', and the show standard 'Summertime'.

Talking of the summer, the band would spend it, as they would the next two, playing almost every festival bill they could sneak their way onto.

As Kelly explained, big outdoor events had their pros and cons. 'You have to walk on without a soundcheck, which means you're holding back; you've got to faff about with the gear because you haven't had a chance to set it up, and you're not comfortable until halfway through your set. But it's a good opportunity to nick other people's fans…'

'I am doing a job that I love doing and getting paid for. I'd give it 10/10. It's tiring as fuck but I wouldn't change it for anything.'

As the late-August release of their first album came into view, the Stereophonics made one of their first major music-press interviews in *New Musical Express*. A double-page spread saw them concentrate on life in Wales, Kelly seeming to be pleased to have made it out! 'At the moment I'm really happy with the way things are. I'm really fortunate to be in a position where I am doing a job that I love doing and getting paid for. I'd give it 10/10. It's tiring as fuck but I wouldn't change it for anything.'

On 17 August 'A Thousand Trees' entered the UK Top 40 at Number 22, an occurrence that landed the Phonics that most treasured of invitations – a ticket to TV's longest-running chart show, *Top Of The Pops*. With just a few days to the release of their debut album there couldn't have been a better time to appear. Presenter Jamie Theakston seemed quite overcome: 'That was the Stereophonics: and they are going to be *massive*, if there's any justice in the world!'

As if to prove they still had a long way to go, though, the Stereophonics appeared at the Virgin-sponsored V97 festival... bottom of the bill on the second stage! Kelly would later rate the event 'best for booking the bands who are happening at the time. It's typical Branson, really, he just goes full on for what the public want. And he gets everything down to the toilet paper right.'

Branson, who attended the event personally, reciprocated with some much appreciated praise. 'It's very exciting to be here seeing the Stereophonics – our very first signing proves the girls and the guys that we've got at V2 have got very good taste. We wanted to see if we could start the label off with a really credible band and they've got everything we could possibly want. I'm absolutely sure they'll go on to great things.

'I'm certain,' Branson continued, 'that within a year or two they'll be topping the big stage. They're delightful people and that's half the battle of trying to create enormous superstars. If they're really lovely people all the record company staff want to work with them.'

Indeed, the next invitation seeking the pleasure of Kelly, Stuart and Richard's company came from the Virgin empire itself. The Cardiff Megastore in Queen Street was to open at midnight on Sunday 24 August as the band's long-anticipated debut album, *Word Gets Around*, was finally offered for sale. At the stroke of midnight, the doors burst open to admit an 800-strong crowd who rushed in from the rain to clamour for their personally signed copy.

'It's typical Branson, really, he just goes full on for what the public want. And he gets everything down to the toilet paper right.'

The limited edition vinyl version, in a special gatefold sleeve, sold out within minutes, proving that not everybody's gone digital (or maybe they were after the extra album of bonus acoustic tracks), but in all other respects everybody left happy including the band, who had to make an overnight drive to London to catch a flight for Germany the following morning. Stuart was not to be with them on this promotional trip, however, retiring to his sick bed with a kidney infection.

The road was taking its toll, but it was too late for the Stereophonics to stop now.

chapter 5:

WORD GETS AROUND

Maybe it was the fact that four tracks had already made their appearance as singles, and that these had been increasingly well received by the public, but the anticipation level as the debut Stereophonics album approached had been greater than any other album of 1997. *Word Gets Around* was received almost as enthusiastically around the UK as it had been in Cardiff when V2 finally unleashed it on 25 August – and the cover art in itself guaranteed the release wouldn't pass the critics by. The now recognisable logo was there, as expected, but the remainder was a collage that positively demanded analysis.

With the three band members seemingly represented by a mouth, an ear and an eye – or was it the three wise monkeys? – the initial letters of the title, W, G and A, were depicted in sign language. The by-now familiar Stereophonics logo topped the sleeve, while the album's title was, in contrast, hand-written in the same way schoolkids have, over time, played the game of Hangman. A matchstick figure at the top left which keyed into this concept was complete but for one arm, suggesting that the guesser had completed the words just in time to avoid losing their 'life'.

Other recognisable symbols included an 'inflammable' sign (possibly a comment on the music contained within), a calendar and time display, while the cut-up feel of the inner booklet, with its snippets of phone books, local newspaper cuttings is almost a return to the days of punk's do-it-yourself sleeves. When quizzed on the subject, the best former art-school boy Kelly could come up with was: 'The cover is lots of different colours, kind of rainbow-y, and the songs are varied as well. I try to make songs as unpredictable as possible.'

The title phrase *Word Gets Around* was lifted from a line in the closing song, 'Billy Davey's Daughter' – and, when questioned, Kelly explained (somewhat more rationally, this time) why they chose it as the album title. 'Fifty per cent of the album is about the way that rumours spread in a small town, and this line fitted in with that. A lot of it was about rumours and gossip and the way the people talk in a small town, so this fitted in and was easy to say.' The 'hangman' graphic makes a reappearance on the last page of the lyric book where this song's words are presented, the letter 'N' being missing from the title suggesting this song was the last piece of the puzzle.

The music on offer was new, all right, but there was a vibe about it that harked back to Creedence, the Kinks, a touch of Otis Redding in the vocal – in fact, a musical collage of past influences which, in that respect, reflected the cover art. The band had recorded the album in the old-fashioned way, setting up together and playing and recording as if performing live. Obviously, vocals and some of Kelly's extra guitars were overdubbed later, but Stuart wasn't comfortable playing with a metronome pulse or 'click track': 'you don't get that live feel or sound,' he complained. 'We were told to try it,' Kelly elaborated, 'but it didn't work. We just play along and patch up what's fucked – that's as technical as we get!' Certainly, the human touch was most welcome, and *Word Gets Around* was about as far from sterile as you could get!

The songs were brought to the band as acoustic demos Kelly taped on a Dictaphone, a small tape recorder usually used by typists and secretaries. 'I try to do a rough arrangement... then we get together and see what works. I write everything on the acoustic, that's why it's so simple.' The music would be credited to the trio jointly, with Kelly acclaimed as sole lyricist – a neat arrangement that gave each member a healthy share of the songwriting royalties. You'd expect nothing less from the last gang in Cwmaman...

Those full band arrangements didn't take too long to work out since, as Richard stressed, these were numbers they'd lived with for some while. 'For the first record you tend to make it pretty instant... we knew all the songs inside out as we'd been playing them for the past five years.'

If there ever was a song tailor-made to open the band's first album, then 'A Thousand Trees' has to be it. Building from the first strumalong chords and Kelly's vocal, it sets the mood and simply builds... And, by making its point in just a fraction over three minutes, it would set the tone for an album that wouldn't outstay its welcome. Like all the songs here, it started life in an acoustic version, played on what its owner described as 'a second-hand, 60 quid Tanglewood guitar.'

'We try to draw emotions out of somebody, rather than appealing to one kind of audience. If you can appeal to everybody from 15 to 50 then you're gonna last a lot longer.'

However you play it, 'A Thousand Trees' tells a sad tale indeed. The subject was a football coach who'd taught Kelly, his older brother and their parents' generation. 'He's about 70 years old, this well respected guy, and they built these gates up for him in the ground and put his picture in the club.' Sadly, this local legend was the subject of accusations of abuse from two girls, and the scandal this created split the village right down the middle. 'It went to court and he was convicted. But he'd built all this up, and then this incident just burned him down...' The tabloids build up sporting heroes and knock them down as a matter of course – as do the music press – but this was somewhat closer to home.

The title of the song had been spotted many years earlier by Kelly as a proverb on the back of a box of matches, and had been stored up in the back of his mind for future use. The written-out lyrics paint the picture fairly clearly, but over the years, he's lost count of the number of people at concerts who think it's about 'Greenpeace or rain forests. It's sarcasm, that's the way we speak where we come from, but a lot of people don't get it.'

Almost anything from this album could be viewed as a potential hit... providing radio would get on board and give the Stereophonics' music that much-needed exposure. Kelly explained the secret of satisfying both the singles and album-buying public. 'We try to draw emotions out of somebody, rather than appealing to one kind of audience. If you can appeal to everybody from 15 to 50 then you're gonna last a lot longer.'

The inspiration for 'Looks Like Chaplin' also hit when Kelly was 12 and his street got flooded. 'The cars were under water,' he recalls, 'with boats going about above them.' Then a junior boxer, he fetched down a punch-bag to act as a sandbag to keep the front door shut – and admits 'I remember having a piss in our hallway, just because I could!' The sinuous bass of Richard Jones provides this song with its backbone, especially as Kelly strains to reach the high notes. The time of nine fifteen referred to in the lyric is reflected by the digital clock on the album cover, but as with that sleeve design this would remain one of Kelly Jones' more enigmatic lyrics.

'More Life In A Tramp's Vest' was applauded by *Kerrang!* magazine for showing the Stereophonic sense of humour, something that separated them from the Manic Street Preachers of this world. Indeed, it's doubtful James Dean Bradfield ever served on a market stall, where this song came together... probably on the back of a brown paper bag! It was, purely and simply, an exercise in observation.

Kelly saw himself as part of a storytelling tradition: indeed, many critics were already comparing him with Welsh bard Dylan Thomas of *Under Milk Wood* fame. And '...Tramp's Vest' was the kind of song that suggested they were on the right lines. 'A lot of what I write about is observations of people, observations of life. I try to make ordinary life to seem special. Ray Davies did a lot of kitchen sink stuff from the old English film. It was an ordinary thing going on, everything was very

normal and ordinary, and nothing was special. But there was always something underneath all that stuff – and that's basically what we're trying to do.'

Musically, there were traces of the Kinks in their mid-1960s heyday, but the biggest audible influence was 'Itchycoo Park' hit-makers the Small Faces. Like their lead singer, the late, great Steve Marriott, Kelly had all the cheek and charm to carry off the most outrageous lyric – and you can imagine Marriott and Ronnie Lane having fun working the word 'cauliflower' into the lyric.

Like 'A Thousand Trees', 'Local Boy In The Photograph' was another tragic small-town tale born from actuality. 'I used to play football with this kid when I was 14,' Kelly told *Kerrang!* magazine. 'One day he came into the shop where I was working and asked about train times. The next day his photo was on the front of the local paper. He'd jumped under a train. That's not something you forget.' *New Musical Express* considered the song to be 'as beautiful as a beery mess can be at closing time, the story of a suicide, a wasted life amplified into a rousing symbol for the inevitable passing of youth.'

Some months later, Kelly was introduced to the father of the lad concerned when they were both in a club in his home neighbourhood. Though he was half-anticipating a glass in the face, or even an invitation outside, the songwriter was relieved to hear the man liked the song and considered it a tribute to his boy. Such, one supposes, are the hazards of writing from real life. The music boasted a churning riff that powered along like the express train that 'runs on and on... past the place they found his clothing'.

'Local Boy...' had come to Kelly when he was just 18. 'I don't know where that came from. Everybody in a small town never talks about themselves, they're always listening to everybody else talking about each other. If you talk about yourself they think you're too important. You never tell anybody your secrets, how you're feeling. You listen to everybody else, hopefully they're worse off than you are. That's where your stories come from. Sixty per cent of "Word Gets Around" is about people either topping themselves or doing something stupid because that's what everybody was talking about in the pub.'

Not surprisingly, given the title, the lyric for 'Traffic' came to Kelly while he was sitting in a traffic jam and spotted a woman in the car next to him. His imagination went for a walk, and came back with a stream of consciousness lyric that came close to word association. 'I just tried to come up with as many scenarios as possible. Is she a slag? Is she a prostitute? Is there a body in the boot? It's about the whole fascination of not knowing who you're talking to.' This was a song that had the capacity to reach outside the band's rock audience, and they'd later discover it was the track that introduced them to another Welsh music legend – albeit one of rather longer standing than themselves – in Tom Jones.

'Not Up To You' saw Stuart's often overlooked musical contribution highlighted as some curiously metronomic drums came to the fore. The reviewer for *The Times* insisted that 'Cable's drum patterns breathe life and momentum into the song,' but in terms of what we'd experienced and what was to follow this came as something of a mid-set, mid-tempo lull. A lyric that was probably one of the less evocative of the album played second fiddle to the almost metallic guitars and a rasping Jones vocal. It seemed typical that the song faded away with the same insistent beat resounding in your ears – and while 'Traffic' had passed the four-minute mark with effortless ease, 'Not Up To You' could have done with a minute pruned off it.

Time for the second set, and 'Check My Eyelids For Holes' opened it with all the impact of 'A Thousand Trees'. The lyrics – minimal in comparison with some of Kelly's songs – meshed perfectly with the music, the trio romping through the song in a shade under two and three-quarter minutes.

Title-wise, it's an expression Welsh people use when they're accused of going to sleep on the job. Yet, as Kelly explains, the subject-matter concerns the kind of things that should be keeping you awake nights. Everybody gets obsessed about losing weight at some point in their life, while 'I swallow honey' is a singer's remedy for sore throats – something Kelly's more than acquainted with. Then, 'the blow job part', as Kelly describes it, 'is about whether you should get back together with someone and whether her giving you a blow job changes anything.' The age-old on-off relationship problem... there's nothing so universal.

How to describe 'Same Size Feet'? A breath of fresh air would do for starters, the acoustic intro giving way to the full band treatment. A very dark lyric revealed the fact that Kelly's main influences in penning the album were current TV drama classics like Jimmy McGovern's *Cracker*, *Hearts And Minds* and *Our Friends In The North*. '*Pulp Fiction* was a major thing for me as well. Every story had a twist at the end.' Suffice to say the title, 'Same Size Feet', refers to a corpse found in a lake...

'Last Of The Big Time Drinkers' deals with the fact that middle-class people think the working classes live to get drunk... little realising they're just as bad. It's written from a post-signing perspective, after Kelly and company had mixed with the movers and shakers of the record industry. 'It's about people working in a factory and just saving enough money to get pissed at the weekend and to have a holiday once a year. They've got no more ambitions – that's just how they live. It's a fact of life. But people in record companies do exactly the same things.'

The circles Kelly now moved in just did it on a different level. The point was hammered home by an Oasis-style rock arrangement and a chorus that could be – and was – taken up by audiences everywhere. Producer Marshall Bird contributed honky-tonk keyboards.

The imagery of 'Goldfish Bowl' brings the listener back to small-town reality, the ace in the hole being the 'burning, sleeping, thieving, cheating' chorus that gives this acoustic-based song its drive. What sounds like an uncredited harmonica solo adds a new musical dimension before Kelly wraps the song up.

'Too Many Sandwiches' was by far the longest of *Word Gets Around*'s dozen selections, clocking in at five minutes and a second. Yet there's little build-up here as the electric riff and rhythm section hammer in together. The setting's a wedding, and grandpa's chucking up after one too many sherries, the wedding singer's chatting up the barmaid, the disco's late and... well, listen for yourself. We've all been there. The metallic overkill of the backing seems to grate, too, after the three-minute mark, but that's quite deliberate.

And so to 'Billy Davey's Daughter', the song whose lyric titled the album and one inspired by a family that apparently lives near to Kelly's brother. 'The story could be the opposite to what happened,' Kelly

confesses. 'By the time the story got to us, we heard that she'd jumped off the bridge. And some people say that she was pushed. I've always found it fascinating how the story changes by the time it gets to you. It could become a better story or a worse one. People exaggerate and add things.'

Musically, it was a masterstroke... following the headache of 'Too Many Sandwiches' with a softly-strummed folksong. Simple chords, moving lyrics, an almost elegiac quality to end the record. The cello obligato, supplied by session musician Nadia Lannman, adds the final, heartrending touch.

Word Gets Around had lasted a shade over 42 minutes, yet had delivered everything a fan could have wanted... and more. It's doubtful that any debut since Oasis's *Definitely Maybe*, three years before, had won such praise and created such impact. And though it may now have been overtaken sales-wise by its successor, *Word Gets Around* continues to deserve its accolades.

Press reaction to *Word Gets Around* was pretty favourable. *Select* magazine, always a champion of guitar bands, gave it a 4/5 review in their September 1997 issue. Scribe Kate Hodges nailed her colours to the mast with the statement: 'The Stereophonics are passionate, honest. They mean it,' before accusing them of moving into Manics territory 'with their corking, intelligent yet chunky stuff.' She then redeemed herself by stating that, though *Word Gets Around* might be 'superficially chock-a-rock, the tear-jerkingly emotional 'Traffic' proves that, underneath the bluster, the Stereophonics have the potential to inspire massed lighter-waving with the best of them.'

Over at *Q* the following month, Martin Aston followed Kate's lead with a generous 4/5 assessment. He attempted to define the band's formula by classing the opening tracks 'A Thousand Trees' and 'Looks Like Chaplin' as combining 'R&B throb, soul ache, American alt-rock thrash and in guitarist Kelly Jones's voice, hollering metal.'

As if to prove the latter statement, *Kerrang!* chimed in with yet another 4/5 verdict, their Paul Elliott offering the following recommendation: 'If you want full on rock action look no further than 'Not Up To You' or 'Too Many Sandwiches'. If it's great songs you're after you won't be disappointed.'

As September 1997 arrived, *Word Gets Around* made its impressive debut in the UK album charts by breaking in at Number 6. The biggest portion of the media spotlight was still being claimed by Oasis, whose third album *Be Here Now* had been released the previous week and remained in pole position, having already sold a ridiculous 1.5 million copies, while positions 2, 3 and 4 were occupied by three classic examples of their genre. Texas's airbrushed pop-soul epic, *White On Blonde*, was still enjoying mega chart action half a year after release thanks to a well-judged succession of hit singles, the Prodigy's *The Fat Of The Land* had spent six of its nine chart weeks at the top thanks to their high-profile videos, while *OK Computer*, Radiohead's third long-player and also a former Number 1, was also showing staying power after coming in at the top three full months earlier.

'We just want to keep the people interested in us, and that's why we play live a lot. We don't want people to forget about us because this business can be so fickle.'

The week's highest new entry was the Levellers' *Mouth To Mouth*, which only just shaded it from the Phonics to reach the Number 5 slot. It would stick around the Top 10 the following week, while *Word Gets Around*, frankly, plummeted like a stone. Its chart positions for the following weeks read 22, 45 and 64 as new albums from higher-powered artists (from Genesis to Mariah Carey and back again) exerted a downward pressure. It seemed the band's fans had bought, and that *Word Gets Around* wasn't going to get around quite enough to turn the Stereophonics from cult heroes to chart contenders with staying power.

We were then into the Christmas silly season... but on 19 December came the announcement that *Word Gets Around* had reached the 60,000 sales figure that would win the band a silver disc. The news was announced

before their 100th gig of 1997 at Cardiff University, where they were presented with their trophy on stage to much pride-tinged embarrassment. But let's not get ahead of ourselves here…

Having successfully launched the album, the band embarked on their first tour of Europe, visiting Scandinavia, France and Germany as well as playing at Reading. It was a hectic touring schedule by any standards. Stuart: 'We just want to keep the people interested in us, and that's why we play live a lot. We don't want people to forget about us because this business can be so fickle.'

The band had, in fact, played their first gig in Germany in Cologne in July, but since only the media – print journalists and radio station DJs – were admitted they didn't really count it as their Deutschland debut. This caused a nice wave of support on which they could now surf, but Kelly was reluctant to be seen as anybody's next big thing. 'In the UK they've got a next big thing every week. It's a joke really. It's a waste of time. I don't know. I think a lot of people are taking the press from Britain and turn it into different things in different countries. I've got no ideas.

'Shallowness is out and songs are back. It's a good time for music... it's a good time for us.'

'I think we're gonna do a lot of work in these different countries, we wanna be established everywhere we go to. And I think we've got the songs to back us up, and we can do gigs. So if they call us the next big thing because we do enough work then we can be. I'm not afraid of that. A lot of bands get called and they don't have songs to back them up. I think we've got the songs to back *us* up.'

The band had, coincidentally, been in Germany when news of the album's success first broke. 'Stuart had glandular fever at the time so he couldn't celebrate,' recalled Richard, 'but Kelly and I certainly did. We were on a promotional tour in Berlin when the phone call came through, (so we) went out and got *slaughtered*.'

Having introduced themselves to Europe in this fashion, the band's next task would be to make their first promotional visit to the United States, where 'A Thousand Trees' was American radio's first taste of the threesome. But in the event Kelly and Richard had to make the trip alone, poor old Stuart – once again the invalid – being stuck in hospital with a kidney infection. Their Stateside adventure had been scheduled to include an appearance at the CMJ Festival in New York, reputedly one of the biggest festivals in the world, but this had to be cancelled.

Scratching a show was an exceedingly rare event in the Stereophonics scheme of things, as Kelly was quick to explain. 'We cancelled one gig out of a hundred or so last year, and we've gained a lot more from all that work than from getting pissed and making headlines (that way). You've got to make a mark first before you can do things like that. I don't think the Who were throwing things out of windows before they had a few albums behind them.

'I wouldn't want to be doing what we're doing at any other time,' he concluded. 'Shallowness is out and songs are back. It's a good time for music... it's a good time for us.'

With a new album to promote, the next step for the Stereophonics was clearly a UK tour, an 11-date jaunt which was scheduled for the end of September onwards. The itinerary stretched from London to Brighton, Scotland, Manchester, Norwich, Port Talbot, Cambridge, Northampton, Leicester and Nottingham. Stuart, for one, was absolutely amazed at the experience of playing to packed houses. 'It's really strange,' he told *Melody Maker*. 'All of a sudden the crowds know every single word to every song and you can't hear Kelly.' The singer was for his part amazed that clubs where they'd played to a dozen people earlier in the year were now selling out, touts asking – and getting – £25 for a ticket.

£25 was ten pounds more than Richard was typically being paid for a day's work 'on the coal' not so many months ago. 'It's really weird,' he confessed. 'You try to take in what happened last year and it's really hard to absorb everything... playing with the Who or flying first class to America.'

There was a real wave of enthusiasm that, alongside the rising stars of Catatonia, underground favourites Super Furry Animals and 60ft Dolls and the already mega Manic Street Preachers, suggested Wales really *was* the place to be. *New Musical Express*'s Steven Wells was, despite himself, impressed. 'They've done for rural South Wales what Bruce Springsteen did for New Jersey,' he said, crediting them with turning 'mundane inside-page headlines unto massive, rampant anthems.' Richard, for one, would be delighted if the London-fixated industry took a trip down the M4. 'They shouldn't be narrow-minded, there's talented bands and good music in rural areas too.' Kelly: 'Problem is there'll be a shitload of crap bands from Wales now, as record companies race after their own Welsh Band...'

'Traffic' was released in late October as the fifth single from *Word Gets Around* to coincide with the band's tour and, boosted by their live performances (as well as *Kerrang!*'s vote for 'Most Beautiful Song of the Year') became the Stereophonics' first Top 20 entry. The single was available in three formats, two CDs and old-fashioned vinyl. CD1 combined the radio edit of 'Traffic' with 'Tie Me Up Tie Me Down' (Kelly borrowing the title from a cult film), 'Coal Chambers' and 'Traffic's full-length album version, while CD2 consisted of four live tracks recorded at their appearance at the Belfort Festival in France earlier in the year. Tracks on this 'Festival EP' were 'Traffic', 'More Life In A Tramp's Vest', 'A Thousand Trees' and 'Local Boy In The Photograph', while the 7-inch vinyl B-side saw 'Tie Me Up...' make a reappearance.

'Problem is there'll be a shitload of crap bands from Wales now, as record companies race after their own Welsh Band...'

The Stereophonics followed their UK jaunt with a tour of Europe, playing their own headlining gigs and supporting Supergrass in Germany before returning home in mid-November for a few days' well-earned rest. Recording sessions then started for their second album, thought at that point to be due for release in July 1998. As it transpired, fans of 'the hardest-working band in rock' would have to wait just a little longer than *that* for their second helpings…

The boys, as well as their fans, certainly had a lot to celebrate after their previously mentioned 100th gig of the year in Cardiff in December, when a special party was organised to mark the end of a highly eventful '97. But the night nearly ended in tears when Kelly arrived with his friends at the after-gig party at a city-centre club. The establishment's bouncers seemingly couldn't be persuaded that Kelly was one of the hosts of the evening's entertainment, and a disagreement apparently ensued.

Happily, MTV presenter Eddy Temple-Morris, a friend of Kelly's (who'd play host at the following year's Cardiff Castle gig and appear in the video of the event), was able to restore order and ensure the singer's admission to join family, friends and the support band, North Star. The party eventually moved on to the foyer of the Angel Hotel, and lasted until six in the morning, making up for time lost.

Following the celebrations, Stuart jetted off to Gran Canaria and came back with both a tan (fine) and a curly perm (unwise); Richard likewise decided a change of image was in order and bleached his hair near-white. Kelly, who admitted having time off was 'strange', simply retreated to the womb-like safety and security of Cwmaman. He revelled in the fact he could still talk to people he knew without them giving him the 'star' treatment. 'They ask lots of questions and you're Terry Wogan for a while,' he admitted, 'but then it gets back to normal and you find out what everyone else has been doing.' And doubtless getting what Del Amitri would call 'Food For Songs' along the way…

The album may have sunk out of sight under a welter of seasonal 'Greatest Hits', but music this good simply would not be denied. Once the Spice Girls, the *Titanic* soundtrack and the rest had finally had their say and 1998 began, *Word Gets Around* was bobbing up once again in the Top 75. By Valentine's Day, 14 February, it had even re-entered the Top 40. *Word Gets Around* could now claim to feature three Top 40 singles – but, as it turned out, 'Traffic' was not to be the last…

chapter 6:
BRITS AND BAFTAS

The new year of 1998 saw the Stereophonics once again back on the bus –
but this time it was the Brat Bus tour, promoted by *New Musical Express*
and sponsored by Miller beer. Also featuring ethnic adventurers the Asian
Dub Foundation, rock hopefuls Warm Jets and female-fronted
Theaudience on an eclectic bill, it opened at Dublin's Red Box club on
13 January, and its UK run climaxed with a 25 January show at London's
Astoria which was simulcast live by Radio 1. The band would then move
on into Europe, Australia/New Zealand and USA/Canada.

The Stereophonics' path to the Astoria through London's minor rock
venues had been a rapid and interesting one. The Monarch pub in trendy
Camden had been followed by the University of London Union, by way
of the Highbury Garage, traditionally a hotbed of indie guitar-bands.
It mirrored the performance of their singles, which had peaked at 51, 33,
22 and 20... a nice upward progression that had been capped by the
Top 10 success of the album. 'Every band has a plan they try to stick to,'
said Kelly, 'but we couldn't believe how tight ours went.'

Rival music paper *Melody Maker* who'd 'discovered' the new sensations showed there were no hard feelings by announcing the Stereophonics as their choice for 'Best New Act of 1997'. The *NME*'s tour organisers had been lucky to persuade the trio to take part, as they'd wanted four weeks off after ten months solid touring, but in the end they were 'nagged into it' and enjoyed the company of such a varied bill.

The road can be a hard place and, though all three Phonics were physically robust specimens, they were keen to look out for their health. 'We didn't expect to have half this work to do,' Kelly explained. 'We've got to be careful, because sometimes we've overdone it. Stuart was very sick at one point because of the workload. We've had doctors in the dressing room; you've got a rash on your leg, he takes your blood pressure, says it's too low and sends you off for vitamin jabs so you can carry on with the tour.'

'When they read out our name, Kelly was up there like a greyhound out of a trap.'

But the biggest news of the month was that the band had been nominated in the 'Best Newcomer' at the 1998 Brit Awards. The category was a much-prized one since, unlike the other prizes doled out by industry fat cats, this was voted by listeners of Radio 1 – ironically a station the band felt didn't give them nearly enough airtime.

Stuart, for one, didn't think they had a chance. 'I remember watching Oasis winning, Kula Shaker and Supergrass. We said years and years ago we'll go there one day for the crack, and now we've been invited. I think someone like All Saints will win, but it's nice to be nominated.' (For the record, the Stereophonics' fellow nominees included not only All Saints but Shola Ama, Finlay Quaye, Olive, Roni Size and *NME* Brat Award winners Embrace. 'When they read out our name, Kelly was up there like a greyhound out of a trap,' laughs Stuart, who revealed that his colleague told him in the hotel 'not to say anything stupid'.

And that was ironic, given that Kelly's acceptance speech – 'About time we got some fucking recognition!' – was brief and to the point: Broadcasters ITV were unhappy about the language and the speech was censored. 'I found it too ironic,' he later admitted, 'that the award was voted for by Radio 1 listeners, yet until our last single they hadn't played any of our records all year. So I was excited, pleased but fucked-off... and I made the mistake of making it public!'

It wasn't as if they hadn't realised what was coming. Stuart had sussed out that the cameras made a habit of hovering round the next act to be honoured, and had spotted the crew shuffling around very conspicuously behind them about five minutes before the award was bestowed!

Coming up with considered words as was his habit, Richard suggested that, as all the shows they did had been sold out, this award was 'one for the fans'. According to their record label V2, the Brits 'sent the Stereophonics into another league, gets them to a lot more people. There was awareness from outside their fanbase but that exposure in one night went from the album selling 60,000 to 200,000.'

The near-miss single 'Local Boy In The Photograph' was re-released in the wake of this success and reached Number 14 – a full 37 places higher than it had managed first time round. The A-side was remixed for radio-friendliness by studio wizard Dave Bascombe and was released in two CD versions plus a cassette. CD1 featured 'Who'll Stop The Rain', an old favourite Creedence Clearwater Revival song from Tragic Love Company days destined to appear in the Channel 4 film *The Girl With Her Brains In Her Feet*, and the 'Local Boy In The Photograph' video. CD2 also featured video footage for fans with PCs, this time a version of 'Traffic' shot in their home town, plus another delve back into the cover-version archives for the Eagles' 'The Last Resort'. An extra bonus here was a live version of 'Not Up To You' which was broadcast by London's independent radio station XFM in September 1997.

Meanwhile, 'World Gets Around' was on the up and up again, benefiting from the band's new-found fame. Having re-entered the Top 20, from which it had dropped in its second week of release, in February 1998, it would spend two more weeks in the 20. It then sunk into the 60s but grimly refused to leave the Top 75 as the year progressed, and apart from a fortnight's 'summer holiday' in June would remain a chart item all the way through to October.

Meanwhile the Brit statuette took up residence on Stuart Cable's hi-fi at home in Cwmaman. The whole village had been huddled round their radios – the event being televised in edited (and censored!) form the following night, a safeguard introduced a decade ago after the shambolic ceremony hosted by Samantha Fox and Mick Fleetwood. Early mentor Graham Davies was one of those back home lending an ear from afar and 'wondering if the boys would do well. And when they won, we all went and had a party.' No change there, then…

More appearances followed on *Top Of The Pops, TFI Friday* and *The Big Breakfast* before band and label alike set their sights on further-flung horizons – the US for a month (their second Stateside tour) and Australia for three weeks. A sell-out show at Sydney's Metro was the highlight of the latter jaunt which the press dubbed 'South Wales comes to New South Wales'! The jaunt was rounded off by a quick over-water hop to New Zealand, where they played an 18 April gig at Auckland's Power Station.

We don't know if Kelly, Richard and Stuart kept diaries – but there were certainly enough camera lenses pointed in their direction to record their every move. The Sydney show two days earlier had been filmed in its entirety for MTV's *Live & Direct* show, the venue's capacity of 1,200 underlining the popularity of the band on their first trip Down Under. While they were away in April, BAFTA (the British Academy Film & Television Awards) gave them an award for *The Slate*, a documentary filmed back in January 1997.

The cameras of BBC Wales had also been following the boys around of late, and a new documentary programme was shot that would hit the nation's screens in late July. *A Family Affair* not only charted the band's rise to fame but included interviews with members of the boys' families.

Showbiz hobnobbing over, the Stereophonics took a welcome week's break before packing their bags in late April and hopping over the border to Bath. Ex-Genesis singer Peter Gabriel's RealWorld Studios were the destination, the intention being to continue recording of the follow-up album which was now scheduled to be released in early 1999. These recordings sessions would last for six weeks and see a number of future favourites committed to tape.

Cutting another album was something the band, though keen tourers, were more than eager to do. 'The record company wanted us to keep on plugging the first album – but we'd have ended up touring another two years.' Though there were one or two exceptions, most notably 'She Takes Her Clothes Off' which had been written in 1995, the songs they brought with them had largely been written while on tour. 'As soon as we stopped recording the last album we started to write the next,' Kelly commented, adding darkly 'If you stop and think you've got a year to write the next one, you're fucked.'

They'd take a break from the studio in May for a very special assignation that brought the trio of red-blooded Welshmen face to face with their Prince. Charles Windsor had tried to get involved with the nation's youth via the Prince's Trust, helping those with few prospects improve their lot. He showed a lot of common-sense, too, in recruiting rock stars to help get the message across, but the image had very much been Chas, Di and Dire Straits or Phil Collins – Status Quo had been about as 'far out' as the Royal rocker had seemed willing to venture. Now it was time for a new approach, and the Stereophonics were happy to be involved.

Ironically, when the band's PA system had been stolen while touring early on in their career, and the Prince's Trust had helped them out of a tight spot. Their subsequent success suggested the charity was spending its money effectively.

Big names from outside the world of pop attending the invitation-only event included Kevin Spacey, Joanna Lumley, Ben Kingsley, Ben Elton, Stephen Fry, boxer Prince Naseem Hamed and TV presenter Melvyn Bragg – a *South Bank Show* in the making, perhaps? The Stereophonics played 'Looks Like Chaplin' and 'Traffic' to the celebrity audience as a thank you to the charity for their support, and certainly went down a storm with actor Spacey (best known for *The Usual Suspects* and *LA Confidential*). In July, in fact, he'd invite the threesome round to dinner in his English home to swop stories of California and Cwmaman.

It was around this time that the band announced their biggest headlining gig to date. It would take place on 12 June at Cardiff Castle, a venue previously used only by the highest-flying bands on the block: Queen (20 years ago, with Thin Lizzy supporting) and the Rolling Stones had been their two and only predecessors. A sell-out crowd of 10,000 was expected for what was immediately (and with apologies to 1970s hitmakers Slade) dubbed 'Cwmaman Feel The Noize'. The Castle had been the imaginative alternative to performing two gigs at Newport Centre as a way of showing their appreciation to the local fans who had given them their first leg-up to fame – and crowning what had been an amazing couple of years with something very special.

The boys knew they were popular after the success of their early-year touring... but even so, the rate at which tickets passed across counters astounded and delighted them. 'We just thought we'd give it a crack,' said a gobsmacked Stuart, 'we never thought we'd do ten days, a thousand tickets a day, sold out. It's nice for us all because we know now that those 10,000 people have come to watch us.' The gates for the event opened at 5.00pm, with support acts Warm Jets (who'd impressed the Phonics on the

Brat tour) and SubCircus warming up the crowds from 6.30pm.

Family and friends had made the short journey up from Cwmaman to see the boys. 'It was really amazing, I was so proud when I saw them there,' an emotional Mabel Cable told Radio 1. 'I was a little bit worried in case anything awkward occurred, but it didn't. The fans were fabulous, absolutely *fabulous*. I'm proud of them as well.'

And that audience took many of the words out of Kelly Jones's mouth, singing lustily and word-perfect to 'A Thousand Trees' and bringing a lump to many a throat. 'This guy from Cwmaman was playing the Bush six months ago,' remarked an awe-struck Graham Davies, 'and all these kids know the words to his songs – it was amazing.' Little wonder Kelly finished the gig, which included the debut of a new song, 'The Bartender And The Thief', by thanking the fans with a jaunty 'Never a chore, always a pleasure!'

'I never knew their fans idolised them so much until I saw 10,000 people singing along to obscure B-sides.'

Stuart rated the experience the gig of his career so far. 'Unbelievable, 10,000 people singing louder than the PA – our soundman was really struggling. Wales is the land of song, and it lived up to its name tonight!' Kelly pointed out that, while continental audiences were quieter and listened a lot more intently, which was flattering to any songwriter, sometimes 'you just want a rowdy crowd like Cardiff... it was cool.'

Journalist Darren Broome of BBC Radio Wales had been an unbeliever when he came down to record some soundbites for a programme on the band. He left a total convert. 'I never knew their fans idolised them so much until I saw 10,000 people singing along to obscure B-sides,' he commented. 'People are *seriously* passionate about them.' Next to him, 20 year old fan Nick Skinner was happy to explain why he rated the Cwmaman three above the Manics. 'I love the Stereophonics because they're not full of all that political shit.'

The momentous concert would be voted 'Best Live Event of 1998' at the Red Dragon Radio Awards in Cardiff, while a video of the show – *Cwmaman Feel The Noize – Stereophonics Live At Cardiff Castle*, released by Visual Entertainment and containing four previously unheard songs – would be nominated for a Welsh BAFTA. 'Elsewhere in Cardiff,' commented a clearly impressed *New Musical Express*, 'hundreds of EC politicians have gathered to broker deals. But they'll never hope to articulate this kind of union in the castle grounds, as three blokes turn the delirium of 'More Life In A Tramp's Vest' into a monumental, noisy accord.'

'Whenever it rains at festivals, it can go either way. It can be really dull, or people just think "Fuck it, let's enjoy it", and get into it even more.'

It was also confirmed that the Stereophonics would be playing at Glastonbury, the Virgin-sponsored V98 in Leeds and Chelmsford and Scotland's T In The Park in the summer. But proposed European Festival dates in France and Switzerland were placed in jeopardy when two of the Stereophonics members got into physical difficulties. The ever-unfortunate Stuart sustained a suspected broken ankle while playing park football, an injury which temporarily put him on crutches – but as if that wasn't serious enough for a drummer, Richard was the victim of an altogether more frightening assault that took place on 4 July outside his local pub, the Rock in Aberaman, after having been accused of damaging his assailant's mother's car.

'Having my face beaten against the floor was pretty fucking weird,' Richard later admitted. 'I got a broken nose, ribs, cheekbone, fingers, wrist – stamped on and everything.' He'd at least anaesthetised himself first with half a bottle of tequila, celebrating the band's return from a flying visit to Japan where they'd played on the slopes of Mount Fuji – but to set off for home and wake up two hours later in hospital was no fun whatsoever. 'The biggest shock was people's reaction... Kelly and Stuart couldn't even recognise me, and my girlfriend (Donna Jones) screamed her head off!' His assailant was put away for six months after the case was heard in December 1998.

Richard's mother Mairwen was glad the attacker got his just desserts. 'My son was so badly beaten his face was unrecognisable,' she said. 'Richard and the boys have been doing fantastic things, but this attack could have ended his career, and that would have been a tragedy.' It was ironic that Richard, who'd admit he was the one of the trio who'd be found most often in fights in his younger days, was now to be found on the tour bus up to his nose in books on Tibetan Buddhism...

As it transpired, the band soldiered on and played the scheduled dates despite their many problems. The Chelmsford leg of V98 had the misfortune to be held on a particularly wet day, which could have been an anticlimax, but the crowd's spirits failed to be dampened. 'Whenever it rains at festivals,' Kelly observed, 'it can go either way. It can be really dull, or people just think "Fuck it, let's enjoy it", and get into it even more.'

August was usually a quiet month in the rock'n'roll calendar, but not so for Stereophonics. Having planned to continue recording, they found an invitation on their collective doormat to attend the *Kerrang!* Awards. The magazine was famed for its dedicated coverage of the heavy metal scene, but had broadened its outlook in the 1990s to encompass quality rock – and the Stereophonics were certainly that.

Kelly could remember delivering the magazine to 'all the cool kids on the street' when he was a paperboy – especially because they used to give away fabric patches to sew on the back of your Wrangler jacket, as was the fashion. The best new band in Britain would add a third statuette to their mantelpiece when they took the honours in the 'Best New British Band' category. The man presenting the award was singer Tony Wright of Terrorvision who were the first band ever to win it. 'This year we're going to lend it to the Stereophonics,' the ebullient Yorkshireman leered – but even before the envelopes had been opened and the results announced, all were agreed it was well worth interrupting the recording sessions for.

It had been a big enough thrill in itself to spy one of their all-time heroes, AC/DC's diminutive guitarist Angus Young, sitting just a few tables away from them along with singer Brian Johnson – a fact Kelly, untypically almost lost for words, referred to in his touchingly impromptu acceptance speech. 'This is a bit of a strange one,' he stammered, 'because all I can think about is when I was eight years old and Richard was eight years old and we went to a fancy dress party as Angus and (brother) Malcolm Young. And there Angus is sitting in the corner…' After introductions had been made over a drink, Kelly commented: 'That's gotta be destiny, innit? Only Jack Nicholson left – I'll have met all my heroes then.'

In the autumn, when the Stereophonics made a return visit to Australia, they'd take fan worship to great lengths indeed by paying a respectful visit to the grave of original AC/DC wild man, Bon Scott. One of the legendary wild men of rock, Scott had died in London in 1980 while sleeping off an all-night binge in a car (the band had been known to dedicate 'Last Of The Big Time Drinkers' to him on stage). One of his tattoos had been of a parrot… and, as Kelly and company stood by the grave, a similar bird was sighted perching in a nearby tree. Was this a sign? Hard to say… but nice to think so.

Word Gets Around had been a highly successful debut album for the Stereophonics, assisted in no small measure by the five singles that appeared on it. Each, of course, had been assigned its own promotional clip, and the early-June release of a compilation video rounded them all up in satisfactory fashion for fans' enjoyment and education. It also featured previously unseen footage plus interviews with band members, but perhaps the most eagerly awaited element was a visual accompaniment for 'Not Up To You', which was released in early 1998 as a single in France. With a running time of 40 minutes and a retail price of £13.99, the video version of *Word Gets Around* was a must for all Phonics fans and fairly flew off the shelves.

The video's release seemed to close a chapter. As 1998 moved towards its close, the question was… what next?

chapter 7:

HOME ARE THE HEROES

'So far so good' might have been the Stereophonic school report for their career so far. Yet the history of rock music is littered with bands whose first album takes the world by storm, yet can't follow up with anything nearly as impressive. There are several reasons for this. The first album is often the cream of the songs the band had stockpiled during their formative years; anything unused then is unlikely to be good enough now.

Another factor is the unremitting demands of the music business. As the Stereophonics had already found, any record label will insist the band travels the world to promote their music in any and every possible market. All this travel can make it hard to be creative – unless, like Kelly, you're adept at writing in hotel rooms, a legacy of the 'brown paper bag' days at Aberdare market. Time for recording sessions is one thing, time for songwriting quite another...

The first proof of what the Stereophonics had up their sleeve came on 9 November 1998 with the release of a new single. 'The Bartender And The Thief' would appear on the forthcoming *Performance And Cocktails* album, now scheduled for release in March the following year. Following the success of the midnight signing session at Cardiff's Virgin Megastore for *Word Gets Around*, it was decided to hold a repeat performance – few bands would wreck their beauty sleep to promote a single, let alone be certain there'd be a sizeable walk-up crowd to greet them.

Inevitably, all expectations were fulfilled – so much so, in fact, that the Megastore had to be temporarily closed. The band had scheduled in two hours to meet their fans and sign copies of the single, but such were the hordes of fans clamouring at the doors that some were inevitably going to be disappointed that they couldn't meet the band. It was a gratifying sign that hinted of successes to come. If things were this manic for the release of a single, what on earth would the response to the album be like?

'This is definitely a "fuck me" moment, you write a song in your bedroom, and a few months later there are people running about beside the River Kwai filming a video for it.'

Kelly looked on the signing as symptomatic of the relationship the Stereophonics enjoyed with their fans. 'We just wouldn't leave until most people had gone – it's the way we were brought up. And yet that's probably the thing that will screw us up, because there's got to be a point where you say no, and walk away.'

Additional tracks on CD1 included two new songs, 'She Takes Her Clothes Off' and 'Fiddler's Green', while CD2 comprised three live tracks – the title song, 'Traffic' and 'Raymond's Shop' – from the Cardiff Castle show. The latter title had originally been a bonus track from the 'Tramp's Vest' reissue that turned into a stage favourite. Midweek sales indications placed the new single at Number 2, with all the prospects of a Top 5 hit when the charts were finally announced on Sunday. Stuart, for his part, couldn't understand why things had suddenly taken off with this, of all records. 'I thought 'Traffic' was going to be huge,' he said, 'I really thought housewives would cotton on to it. And then we write a song full of heavy guitars about lesbians, bartenders and pinching money and it gets to Number 3!'

This new single from a new album marked a real step forward in the band's video aspirations. Having proved their commercial worth, they now commanded bigger budgets and had producers fairly clamouring at their door to work with them. On this occasion, they'd visited Thailand where they took part in a bizarre military ritual on the banks of the River Kwai, the like of which the locals hadn't seen for over 50 years. 'This is definitely a "fuck me" moment,' declared Kelly. 'You write a song in your bedroom, and a few months later there are people running about beside the River Kwai filming a video for it.'

'I tuned all the guitars like Soundgarden and thought I gotta find a riff here'

The concept of the video was borrowed from the film *Apocalypse Now*, where *Playboy* magazine flew Bunny Girls to Vietnam in a helicopter to entertain the troops. 'We're playing the Bunny Girls,' explains Kelly, 'and there's going to be bombs in the river and people shooting at us. None of this has anything to do with the song, but it should look good.' It would prove the first of a number of movie-related videos that would bring the Stereophonics acclaim as cutting-edge video producers and attract the attention of many potential followers from outside their existing fanbase.

They'd also had fun away from the film set, being accompanied everywhere they went by a gaggle of kids who'd met them at the airport at six in the morning and clearly had no other plans for the day. But Kelly found 'heaven' in a place called the Kiss Bar, dedicated to the face-painted US band of that name and decorated in suitably over the top style, where girls danced round poles to the accompaniment of loud, heavy rock. 'It was like a Motley Crue video,' he smilingly recounted.

'The Bartender And The Thief' had, Kelly revealed, come together out of something like desperation – because the new album material he'd written was far too mellow for his liking, with only three real rock songs aboard. 'I tuned all the guitars like Soundgarden and thought I gotta find a riff here…' They went into the studio and, within five 'takes', had come up with the basic track, Richard and Stuart supplying exactly what Kelly had in mind. Even so, 'I never, *ever* thought it would be the first single!'

Maybe it showed how far the band had come that their new release featured in the betting for the top Christmas single, a position which in the last two years had been monopolised by the Spice Girls and which, in any case, was some weeks away from being decided. It's not known if any of their fans took the 50-1 odds… but Richard bet on it hitting Number 1 'for a laugh'. Kelly admitted that when they'd released the single they thought it might be 'too heavy' for radio airplay, and that references to lesbians in the lyrics might do it no favours airplay-wise. 'But we got really good radio and TV support and we've been out there touring loads, so it's all fallen into place.'

The other aspect in the single's favour, according to the Phonics singer, was the preponderance of 'crap on the radio like Steps and B*witched that gave us an advantage. Our song had to be played because it was the only contrast to the rubbish pop stuff – and for once it worked in our favour.' The song bowed at Number 3, beaten only by Steps and 'Believe', the non-moving marathon chart-topper from Cher.

As they'd shown with their Prince's Trust involvement, the Stereophonics were happy to lend a hand when charitable opportunities presented themselves – and did just that on 3 October when another big benefit gig at Llangollen International Pavilion saw them on a bill that included the Crocketts and the Levellers. The whole event was broadcast live on BBC Radio Wales, and the invitation had come from Mike Peters, former lead singer of the Alarm, who in some ways had been the 1980s counterparts of the Stereophonics.

The gig was to raise funds for the conservation of Snowdonia, a campaign to which Hannibal Lecter himself – actor Sir Anthony Hopkins – had lent his not inconsiderable support. The band were also

pleased to do it because, so fast had their rise to fame been, that they'd not played many gigs in the north of the country. (The Alarm, by contrast, hailed from Rhyl and were the area's local heroes.)

The success of 'The Bartender And The Thief' was just the fillip the boys needed as they tore into another nationwide tour – and, not content with storming the country in their own right, they also announced a support slot with James on their end of year shows which ran from 5 to 14 December. Many bands would have turned their noses up at returning to opening-act status at this stage, but with venues like Birmingham's NEC and Glasgow SECC on the itinerary it was an ideal chance to 'steal fans', festival-style – not to mention give people who missed out on tickets for their October/November jaunt a second chance to get in on the live action.

And so it proved at Birmingham, where the tour opened. The last time Kelly had graced this cavernous Exhibition Centre venue was as an audience member, watching (who else but) AC/DC; he still had the ticket stub! Instead of the luxurious chauffeur-driven car that sped him there this time, he'd shared a minibus with a number of pissed pals who had thoughtfully brought an empty barrel with them to serve as a portable toilet. His thoughts, on seeing the venue again (and locating the seat he'd sat in those years before), were that 'people said two years ago we'd be playing places like this come the Millennium.' Everything, it seemed, had happened a full 12 months ahead of time.

New songs were already in the set, with the album having been done and dusted as early as June but being kept under wraps to let the Christmas rush go by. Kelly was pleased to have the chance to introduce them gradually into the set and see how they were received compared to the tried and trusted *Word Gets Around* favourites. 'We started doing them in France, where they went down really well. They're going to be 13 songs on the album spanning one extreme and another; the harder stuff is *much* harder…'

Many of the headlining group's fans started the Stereophonics set in the bar, doubtless repulsed by the usual tape of AC/DC hits that preceded the Phonics' appearance on stage (well, it made Kelly feel at home…). Maybe some of them had, like the band, taken a sneak peep at the BBC's *Clothes Show Live* exhibition in one of the next-door arenas. But, during the course of the very first number, seats would miraculously fill, the bars would empty and James' audience were there – ripe for the picking!

Once upon a time, the band would have been fazed, overawed by an audience this size. Now it was just another day at the office, the rhythm section chatting absent-mindedly between (and even during) songs as Kelly addressed the audience. By the time the Stereophonics hit the home stretch of their 50-minute set, not only had the NEC crowd been well and truly warmed up, but a large proportion of the 10,000 people present were making a mental note to put *Word Gets Around* on their Christmas present list.

'The music inspired the audience to dance in a particular way... the entire audience was bouncing up and down in usual, putting an unusual strain on the sprung floor.'

Television was also on the agenda, as ever, and the trio played the usual round of shows including *The Ant & Dec Show,* MTV's *Up For It, Top Of The Pops* and *TFI Friday.* Not that they felt Chris Evans was doing them any favours. 'If you look at (1960s pop programme) *Ready Steady Go!* and all that, the acts used to entertain and enjoy it,' said Kelly. 'Watch *TFI Friday* now and everybody's as stiff as a board – they don't want to do it.' Though they'd continue to play for the new owner of Virgin Radio (presumably a man who should be obeyed in the record company's eyes), they certainly wouldn't brown-nose him. 'Chris Evans talks to guests soon enough if Alanis Morrisette's playing,' grumbled Stuart good-naturedly.

It wasn't unknown for a Stereophonics fan to claim that their music made the earth move for them, but an incident in Edinburgh during the band's tour was nearly no joking matter. The 900-capacity Assembly Room was packed solid, and people were really starting to enjoy themselves when cracks appeared in the floor in front of the stage. Kelly stepped up to the microphone in a bid to calm things down. Proceedings were interrupted for a time – but, after an inspection by the local council, the okay was given for the show to continue. 'The Stereophonics played their full set and no-one was hurt,' confirmed a spokesman for the band, adding: 'There was a feeling that both the band's quick response to the problem and the audience's reaction may have averted a nasty incident.'

Eyewitnesses claimed the ceiling in the room below where the audience were jumping around was cracking, with plaster raining down – a reaction explained thus by a council spokeswoman: 'The music inspired the audience to dance in a particular way, which meant that virtually the entire audience was bouncing up and down in usual, putting an unusual strain on the sprung floor.'

Having rocked Scotland's capital to its very foundations, and returned to Japan for a brief headlining tour, the Stereophonics cemented their relationship with Welsh rugby in November when they were invited to play a two-song set – 'The Bartender And The Thief' and 'A Thousand Trees' – at Wembley Stadium, where 75,000 were about to watch Wales take on South Africa. Yet, if truth be told, only Stuart of the trio was anything like a rugby fanatic; the round, rather than the oval, ball was uppermost in Kelly Jones' thinking.

The Stereophonics happened to be in London appearing on the *Ant & Dec Show* on Saturday morning TV, which scuppered plans to see Liverpool playing Leeds United. 'We couldn't make it to Anfield in time, so when we saw Wales were playing we phoned up for tickets.' They were then asked to sing for their supper... or, rather, mime to the recorded versions, which was in many ways worse than playing live. 'We've never really done it before,' Kelly explained. 'The music was played over the tannoy and we just stood there playing along.'

The boys had been heartened by the fact that the majority of people in the ground that day were going to be Wales fans who'd streamed up the M4 to watch their exiled side in action, the Cardiff Millennium Stadium replacing the Arms Park still being under construction. Nevertheless the trio worried about facing such a number of non-fans who might not even be into music, full stop. 'It's going to be a shock to a few of 'em.

"What the bloody 'ell are they doin 'ere? It's a rugby match"...' But it wasn't that bad after all. Even better, Wales were inspired by the pre-match performance to take the World Champions close, racking up a creditable 20 points, and it was only in the closing minutes that the Springboks made their superiority tell by reaching a winning total of 28.

The band had been allocated seats in an executive box but, rather than watch in privileged company from behind glass, they elected to move forward and sit outside with their pals, the road crew. 'It took the record company a long time to understand,' said Stuart, 'if we get invited to a party, *they* get invited to a party.'

The following month would see the Stereophonics return to their native Wales for a series of Christmas shows: the first two were at the Newport Centre, playing to 2,000 people each night, while the last was at Cardiff's 6,000-capacity International Arena. They'd not played Newport for three years, so it was no surprise the capacity crowd was gagging for it. And the group could well recall the earlier gig, at the tiny Filling Station, when, as previously recounted, Stuart's camper van tried its best to break down on the way home.

The biggest cheer of the night at Cardiff came when Kelly launched a pertinent question from the stage: 'Are you drunk yet?' With only eight days to Christmas, this lot were getting their celebrations in early, and the community singalong was superb. 'Just cut us away, set us free to float on the world,' smiled an elated Stuart as they trooped off stage to start their own pre-Christmas celebrations.

The *Western Mail*'s rave review of the evening's proceedings the following day concluded that, once Cardiff's much-vaunted Millennium Stadium was completed, 'you can confidently wager that the first band to transform it from a rugby shrine to a bona fide rock venue will be the Stereophonics.' This was one man who'd clearly been at Wembley...

It wasn't only the audiences that had got larger in the Phonics world these days; they now boasted an on-stage keyboardist, Tony Kirkham, whose job was to fatten up the sound and cover up for the overdubs which necessarily doubled the guitar parts in the studio along with Marshall Bird's occasional assistance. The newcomer would get short shrift from Stuart, who instantly described him as 'like Warren Beatty in the film

Shampoo, going round with a hairdryer stuck down the front of his jeans.' Welcome to the gang...

The band's last blast of a glorious 12 months came on Christmas Eve when Steve Lamacq, a long-time champion of the band, broadcast a session on Radio 1. The band were in acoustic mode in this case, and two tracks from the evening – 'Not Up To You' and 'She Takes Her Clothes Off' – would appear the following August on a free CD given away with *Melody Maker*.

The new year of 1999 kicked off with European and Japanese promotional tours to let the world know about the forthcoming new album. The video shoot for the next single ('Just Looking', due for release in February) saw the black-clad lads in a Jaguar, registration number CWM ONE – Stuart driving, Richard in the back. It looks like they may be driving to a wedding, but it turns out to be more like a funeral when the car crashes into a river or lake. The final frame sees Kelly bob to the surface from the front passenger seat, leaving many questions unanswered – including did they do their own stunts?

The Welsh always celebrate St David's Day with abandon – but 1999 was to be something different as Radio 1 invited them to play a special concert at the Golders Green Hippodrome in London to be broadcast on 1 March. It was a venue whose stage had been graced by all rock's most legendary footsteps, and the Stereophonics were delighted to play their part in making history... after a seemingly shaky start.

This unaccustomed hesitance could, charitably, have been put down to the fact that this was the band's first live show in the UK since mid-December. Two pre-broadcast warm-up numbers didn't set the woods on fire, but somehow when the 'Transmission' light flared into life so did they. 'Roll Up And Shine' opened proceedings, and it was amazing to think that this set packed full of what sounded suspiciously like greatest hits had taken just a couple of years to compile.

The bar staff had got into the swing of things by wearing leeks in their buttonholes, while the crowd – as ever these days – came equipped with Welsh flags. They also seemed intent on throwing daffodils on stage, a custom last seen in the heyday of the Smiths... whose singer Morrissey was the one doing the throwing (of gladioli, if you want to split hairs).

The crowd's enthusiasm was perhaps not so surprising when you consider Radio 1 had brought competition winners from all over the world in for the gig.

There were to be two more notable tie-ups with the BBC this spring. Radio Wales broadcast *Performance And Cocktails: The Documentary* on 6 March, while almost exactly a month later Kelly would grace BBC TV... not on *Top Of The Pops* with the other lads, but on *Grandstand* dressed as a busker! The occasion was the clash of Wales and England on the rugby pitch, always an emotive affair designed to drag the last drop of patriotism out of all concerned. Kelly, resplendent in floppy hat, black T-Shirt and jeans and playing an acoustic guitar, offered a new alternative Welsh anthem, snappily entitled 'As Long As We Beat The English'. The boys in red did just that the following day, the single-point margin leading to Scotland taking the Five Nations Championship... and ensuring Kelly's reprise of the song on tour at Glasgow's Barrowlands raised the roof off the venue!

It seemed the band were becoming symbols of national pride – and, when Wales decided to celebrate the launch of their National Assembly with an all-star bash in Cardiff, the Stereophonics were among the great and the good who were invited to take part. They accepted with good grace, unlike the Manics whose spokesman declared 'the monarchy is outdated... they just did not want to play in front of the Royal Family.' (After the tabloids had enjoyed their predictable feeding frenzy, Nicky Wire's brother, Patrick Jones, revealed 'the band were in Germany and couldn't be there anyway.')

'You can take the boy out of Wales, but you can't take Wales out of the boy.'

As it happened, Kelly might as well have been in Germany too. A video clip of the band at Cardiff Castle in 1998 performing 'Traffic' was followed by a short speech from the singer: 'You can take the boy out of Wales, but you can't take Wales out of the boy.' Or at least that's what he was scheduled to have said; a lack of sound left the onlookers – the Queen, Prince Philip and Tony Blair among them – bemused on both counts. But this was to pale into insignificance compared with the Morfa experience.

The prospect of a memorable day out was certainly exciting Stuart. 'It's nice the people your age have got something to talk about, because our fathers and mothers have been talking about all these people for years and years and it's been like, "shurrup, you know, one day we'll have something ourselves." Hopefully we can start that again...

'Maybe it'll be one of those days,' he concluded, 'which'll be an "I was there" gig. People will talk about it for many years to come. people will say "I remember when I was in Swansea to see the Stereophonics."'

The run-up to Morfa saw them playing quite an important gig to around 100 people... in BBC's Television Centre, as guests of Jools Holland and his *Later* programme. It wasn't their first appearance, of course, but it was one with tragi-comic overtones. A roadie had attempted entrance with a plastic gun in his luggage — not a wise move in the wake of *Crimewatch* presenter Jill Dando's unsolved and particularly brutal murder. 'It's only plastic and didn't look that realistic,' explained Richard of something that resided on the tour bus for use in schoolboy pranks, 'but they went ballistic (sic) and banned him from the building for two days.'

More fun and games were to be had at Television Centre when someone accidentally closed a sliding door on Kelly's hand. His brother had recently lost a finger while racing motorbikes, and for a brief yet excruciatingly long second while the door was re-opened, the guitarist couldn't feel his digits. Luckily his left hand emerged unscathed, and he was able to give his usual assured performance on 'I Stopped To Fill My Car Up', 'Pick A Part That's New' and 'Just Looking'. These were all titles of tracks on the new album, with which the world was still becoming acquainted. And from its stark black and white photograph cover to the music it contained, this couldn't have been more different to its predecessor. Word had clearly got around... and excitement was at fever pitch.

The final Morfa warm-up at Liverpool's Royal Court Theatre turned out to be anything but. The concert had sold out by word of mouth alone, ensuring that a greater than usual percentage of Phonics die-hards were present to see their heroes go through their paces. A full two-hour performance (no saving themselves for the big day here) kicked off with 'Hurry Up And Wait', while newer songs like 'T-Shirt Suntan' achieved ovations similar to 'Local Boy In The Photograph', suggesting that the band had overcome the 'second album syndrome' and won acceptance of their newer songs to equal those fans were more familiar with.

One fan, cornered by a music-paper reporter on the way out, dubbed the event 'complete madness all the way through', describing how people were being passed over the top of the crowd just as happened in the old days before the mighty terraces of Anfield and Goodison Park were turned into all-seater stadia. 'They couldn't reach the stage and were trying to get as close as they could... the crowd were bouncing up and down all night.'

Thankfully, Merseyside's floors proved more durable than those north of the border. And no cracks had been discerned in the band's second album, either, when it took its bow in March. Party like it's 1999? The Stereophonics had only just started!

chapter 8:

COCKTAIL PARTY

While *Word Gets Around* had been accompanied by a street-level buzz that conformed with its title, the release of *Performance And Cocktails* had been a considerably bigger deal altogether. We're talking window displays in Our Price here, not to mention the inevitable huge queues at the Cardiff Virgin Megastore at midnight on Sunday 7 March when the lads opened the doors to sign copies of their new release.

Fans had been waiting in line since midday, fully 12 hours before, to secure their place, and the near 4,000 people who passed through the re-opened doors at midnight broke the record held, almost inevitably, by the Manics. The Phonics carried on signing till 5.30am, and just a few hours later were to be found in another record shop – this time HMV's Oxford Street flagship. Where once they'd roamed central London's busiest street with their 'jeans money' burning a hole in their pocket, they were now playing a six-song mini-set for 450 fans, 100 invited guests and the listenership of XFM radio, the capital's independent station. Little wonder, with such dedication, 44,000 copies of the album were sold on the very first day of release.

There was every incentive to sell extra copies, too, as the Stereophonics' second long-player was going head to head with US teen sensation Britney Spears and her 'Baby One More Time' album. Having had a Number 1 with the single of the same name, the smart money was on her repeating the feat with this long-playing pile of plastic pop (or maybe that should be 'silicone songs', given repeated press rumours of the teenagers' alleged breast enhancement). But as Kelly pointed out, Britney appealed to the market where pocket-money extended to cassette singles and not much else, remarking that 'Billie did a lot of singles but her album didn't do that well.'

'Most people's second record is shit, but we'd never release a record with a single filler on it.'

The lad would prove to have a wise old head on those young shoulders. Spears would enter the chart at Number 8... higher than Kula Shaker and Van Morrison, but not our heroes. What was even better was that, just as the new album entered the listings (read on to find out exactly where), *Word Gets Around* made a return to the Top 40 at Number 36, clocking up its 50th week in the Top 75. By this time it had been certified gold, with 100,000 copies sold in the UK alone, but was undoubtedly a whole lot nearer to platinum (300,000) status. Yet to give an idea of how the band's profile and appeal had broadened, the new album would go gold on the strength of advance orders alone.

The build-up was certainly intense, Kelly promising 'the rock songs are a lot, lot bigger. But there's a lot of mid-tempo stuff on the record too. It'd be nice if it was *Morning Glory* to *Definitely Maybe* or Black Crowes' *Musical Companion* to *Shake Your Money Maker*. That step from your first to your second record, which doesn't happen any more.' The reason, he explained, was 'because most people's second record is shit, but we'd never release a record with a single filler on it.' The stage was certainly set for something far more substantial than *Word Gets Around Part 2*, even if most fans would have settled for that. Indeed, the singer admitted that he'd even surprised himself with what had been achieved.

Richard happily declared *Performance And Cocktails* was nothing less than 'the record we always wanted to make. With the first record you tend to make it pretty instant, but this one has all the songs we wanted to put on. There's a lot more space musically in this (than *Word Gets Around*), it's more thoughtful and thought-provoking.' As before, the tactic was to record as a band, then go back in and clean up any mistakes or unwanted rough edges. Kelly had certainly been happy with what his colleagues had added to his initial ideas, a state of affairs Richard out down to 'trusting each others' judgement; we were all brought up in the same area and listened to the same stuff.' Great minds think alike, then…

Rabid fans would have heard five of the songs in the stage set already, while record buyers were familiar with two tracks, 'Just Looking' having become the second single release from the album on 22 February; the song would reach Number 4 in the chart. The single featured 'Postmen Do Not Great Movie Heroes Make', a B-side featuring the vocal talents of backroom boy Marco Migliari from RealWorld studios, and the Ray Davies classic 'Sunny Afternoon' which was already a live staple. CD2 included 'Local Boy In The Photograph' and 'Same Size Feet', the two tracks both recorded live at BBC Radio 1 Lamacq live Christmas Party at Maida Vale studios in December. (As previously mentioned, two more tracks from this set would grace a *Melody Maker* freebie CD entitled 'Long Digging, Gone Fishing, Love Drinking'.)

But the remaining highlights were numerous indeed. 'Roll Up And Shine' kicked off the album, as it so often would the live set – a song accurately described by *Melody Maker* as 'AC/DC given a pop makeover'. The lyric, as ever contributed by Kelly, could be considered as an on-the-road, all lads together boozing anthem, but there was more to it than that. In fact, if any track on the album qualified as its title song then it would be this one, as it was inspired by an unconventional New York club called Shine where the Phonics had played in September 1997. On leaving, they were presented with business cards and matchbooks emblazoned with the legend 'Shine – Performance And Cocktails'.

The song was written the month after the band returned to Britain and was recorded at the Courtyard Studios, Oxford, and Peter Gabriel's RealWorld studio in Bath. Musically, Kelly pinpointed this track along with the one that followed, as 'probably the biggest leap forward for me as a guitar player. I was maybe a bit stilted before, but now my playing is a lot looser, a lot scruffier. I think it's just come out of touring for a year and a half; I kept watching other players to see how they did it.' Certainly, while all the songs on *Word Gets Around* had been played in standard EADGBE tuning, 'Roll Up And Shine' saw him tune the strings down a whole tone each to read DGCFAD.

The impact of this first track, with its almost Led Zeppelin-esque full-on attack, was light-years away from (and ahead of) the more polite, punk-pop sound of *Word Gets Around*. This was Rock with a capital R. And there seemed but a millisecond of silence before the next track hammered in with an uppercut of sound to go with its predecessor's punch to the gut. This was an album where the studio was clearly being used to its fullest extent.

Though Bird and Bush had once again produced, another, independent ear had been lent to the all-important mixing process when Al Clay, famed for his work with the Boo Radleys, Therapy? and Del Amitri among others, joined in. The difference, whatever it was, was undeniably audible as the songs fairly jumped from the grooves.

'The band persuaded me they didn't want to make the leap to a big-name producer,' V2's head of A&R Dave Wibberley told trade magazine *Music Week*. 'Bird and Bush are not Svengali producers, they make the band feel comfortable. But we wanted to put them in more experienced hands at the mixing stage.' Kelly agreed: 'I like working with Bird and Bush, but we felt we wanted to spruce things up in the mix.'

Raw, ragged and righteous, the previously aired 'The Bartender And The Thief' would often be announced on stage as 'The Lesbian And The Thief', hinting at the scenario in which it came together. The band were on the other side of the world in New Zealand whiling away time before a flight in the airport lounge – how often have licensed premises been the location where inspiration has struck Kelly Jones, we wonder? The clientele were certainly a sight more outrageous than he'd have observed in Cwmaman. 'There were all these sailors... and lesbians at the bar.'

Kelly thought himself into the bartender's shoes, wondering what it would be like to see everyone change in character as they moved from sober to drunk and back again. 'So I wrote this completely tongue-in-cheek song about the bartender and a thief who is robbing everybody.' As for the title, well you'd never get it on the radio, would you, boyo? The thief, it transpires, is the bartender's wife. 'He picks out all these drunken people, single men and women, and calls up his missus. She's a bit of a lesbian on the side, she flirts with them, eventually robs them, and they split the pot.'

A tune would prove a little more problematical, but was found on a pocket-sized tape recorder Kelly had been carrying with him to catch song ideas before he forgot them. It had been glued to his hip for two years but he'd never bothered to play it back until, stumped for a suitable melody to fit his New Zealand tale, he dug it out and gave the contents an airing. 'The Bartender And The Thief' proved that patience is its own reward, and the result, according to *Melody Maker*, was a 'raucous, frenzied song about crime, booze and lesbian nookie.' And all that in another weird and wonderful guitar tuning known as 'dropped D'!

If you hear an echo of the 1970s in this song, it's probably the guitar, one of whose parts is played through the 'talk box' apparatus that the likes of Joe Walsh, Peter Frampton and, more recently, Bon Jovi have used. This gives what Kelly calls 'a weird wah-wah sound. I wanted the verse to be really hard and the chorus to be melodic and snappy,' he continues. The percussion added to the basic drum tracks also hustled the song along.

If Kelly had to wait around for the completion of that song in April 1998, then 'Hurry Up And Wait' had proved rather more straightforward. Its title came from a phrase his brother used to use on the tour bus... and that often used and abused vehicle is exactly where the song took shape in October/November 1997 as the Stereophonics toured Britain. The lyric was a perceptive sideways glance at the kind of 'lottery philosophy' prevalent in 1990s Britain, with a population that never seemed content with things as they were. Kelly described it as 'a train of thought song based on all sorts of things... waiting for a traffic light to turn green, a kettle to boil, losing your virginity.'

Though on the face of it deceptively simple and acoustic-based, the music to this song was in fact another example of tuning trickery, and that showed exactly how much Kelly had been developing as a player. Not that he was sitting himself down with back copies of guitar magazines. In fact, when the music publishing company sent him the sheet music of the album some months after release, he was sure what was written on the page was 'completely wrong... sorry everyone, I just couldn't begin to explain what it should be. My guitar tech sorts it out...'

Track four, 'Pick A Part That's New', was written during the band's first visit to New York and reflected how they felt about the much-hyped Big Apple – a feeling of profound disappointment, according to lyricist Kelly. 'You go to buy a sandwich and you've already seen the place in *When Harry Met Sally*!' It all came together, appropriately enough, in a New York hotel room in September 1997 when Kelly and Richard were on a promotional trip; it was the time when Stuart had contracted glandular fever and couldn't make the flight. Like its predecessor, 'Hurry Up And Wait', it was recorded at Parkgate Studios in Sussex.

There must be something about hotel rooms, because Kelly dated 'Just Looking' back to a September 1997 visit to Amsterdam, a city notorious for its red light district. The result, explained its lyricist, mused on the difference in expectations between male and female. The line 'I'm just looking, I'm not buying' would go down in Phonics folklore, if not youth culture.

He reckoned later that the song was 'probably the most personal thing I've ever done,' and in that respect started something of trend. It had been written primarily because someone close to him back home had told him the first album lacked any first-person songs. 'They said, you write about other people in extreme detail, but you've not written about yourself. Now I've started doing it, it's become slightly frightening... I'll have to see where that takes me.' Certainly, one of the earlier album's songs had seemed to stir up controversy, with Mr Davey of 'Billy's Daughter' fame reportedly not happy with the attention that particular title had brought to him and his family. The papers said Kelly had apologised...

Along with 'Pick A Part That's New', 'Just Looking' showed a new variety and maturity in Kelly's guitar-playing, one of the band's most distinctive trademarks. 'I tried to change on this record,' he explained to *Guitar* magazine, adding that the previous album had featured 'mainly just

power chords, all strummed.' The two songs mentioned, he elaborated, 'reflect what I was trying to do – have memorable riffs, decent arpeggio parts. Like every songwriter, I tend to use the same chords again and again – so if I hadn't have changed my approach the songs would have started to sound the same.' The folky picking of the intro would be accompanied and augmented by the rhythm section until the full force of the song hit home with possibly the most memorable chorus of the album.

The level of fame the Stereophonics had achieved at this point was clearly weighing on Kelly's mind when he came up with the cleverly titled 'Half The Lies You Tell Ain't True' – though he'd cite the likes of deceased INXS singer Michael Hutchence and disgraced Welsh Secretary Ron Davies as examples of people the media had used and exploited. (There was an echo, too, of 'A Thousand Trees' in humanity's inherent appetite for destruction.)

It's instructive to note, though, that this song came together over three months between July and October 1997; Princess Diana's death happened right in the middle of those dates. Like 'Hurry Up And Wait', Kelly's brother Kevin had unwittingly supplied the title of an uptempo song that really kicked ass.

The lyric behind 'I Wouldn't Believe Your Radio' was another small-town story, but people would get confused about the title. 'It's not that deep a song, it's just got a strange title,' insisted Kelly, who as ever had written the words. The lyric was about men and women fighting to keep material things after relationship break-ups, but the title was 'a phrase from back home, like when someone lies so much you can't even believe their radio.' *Billy Liar* could also have been an inspiration here.

There was an echo of the Stereophonic record player in the lyric's use of the word 'wireless', an old-fashioned 1950s-60s description of transistor radios powered by batteries that didn't need to be plugged in. The tune, Kelly declared, came to him 'in a dream' and was something that had parallels with the Beatles' music: he'd even wanted Stuart to become the Phonics' Ringo and sing it, 'but it ended up a bit high and he couldn't'.

Mabel Cable's boy certainly played his part, though, with an upfront drum part that somehow echoed the first album's 'Not Up To You'. Another possible reference point was the Jam's 'That's Entertainment' from

1981. The song's other claim to fame was that it was the first to be written on a 'new' guitar Kelly had invested in, a Gibson SG made in 1968... six years before the lad was born! The fact that George Harrison was playing a similar instrument in the 'I Am The Walrus' video from the same era only strengthened the Fab Four connection.

You could read John Lennon parallels, too, into 'T-Shirt Suntan' – a somewhat shocking and fairly noisy song about a record company receptionist being shot by a crazed fan refused admittance to see his idol. All the fan wants to do is show off his T-shirt suntan, an image that Kelly took from way back at the pool in Cwmaman where 'everybody liked to show off their white bodies with brown arms.' The song had started life many months earlier with an entirely different set of lyrics about condoms, rejoicing then in the title of 'Rubber Glove'! Possibly not an airplay favourite in that form...

Given that 'Yesterday' was the Beatles' most covered song, you might see yet another Moptop connection in the slightly mournful 'Is Yesterday, Tomorrow, Today' – and the inspiration for the song was Hamburg, the self-same city where the Liverpudlians learned their stagecraft in the seedy Star Club.

In the same way as 'Just Looking' was inspired by Amsterdam, so '...Yesterday...' had been triggered by sympathy for the prostitutes playing their trade on Hamburg's Reeperbahn, the red light district connection being emphasised by stage lighting when the song was performed. Even in an exotic location as Hamburg, the days can run into each other, each as boring as the next. And the twist, as you'd expect in any song Kelly writes, is that he's looking at life from out of that window, not into it...

As with 'Just Looking', this was what one critic termed 'a thoughtful piece about the frustration of accepting your lot in life.' For *Melody Maker*, the song 'further demonstrates Kelly's ability to communicate in a brilliantly direct way, deftly mixing melody and feeling and scooping up the listener in its warm embrace.' This all tied in with what Kelly himself had told the fans to expect, writing-wise: 'a step forward and a step to the side... most of the songs are more chain-of-thought than storytelling.'

'A Minute Longer' was the first such song he'd written in his new house before taking off on tour in January 1998. A slow, almost-country-flavoured number with definite Rod Stewart overtones in the vocal delivery, it conveyed the feeling of not wanting to emerge into the cruel world of the road but stay cocooned from reality. As Kelly put it, 'If something's a pain in the arse, you'll think back to something better.'

Like many great songs, 'She Takes Her Clothes Off' has a lyric that confronts the fact that beauty is really only skin deep... even when you're as good-looking as Kelly Jones. The object of his songwriting skills this time was a woman whose looks had faded with the passing of time; the inspiration, a character from his home town 'who was always rumoured to be a prostitute'. As the song title suggests, the only way for this poor woman to continue attracting attention is to work as a stripper. Then the reality of the situation catches up with her, with a tragic outcome.

'When we started, we just wanted to get into people's faces, and the only way we knew of doing that was with loud songs.'

'She Takes Her Clothes Off' had been around for a long time, having been one of the songs they presented manager John Brand with at the M4 motorway services... a lifetime or so ago. The music of the embryonic, 1995-era track was originally much faster and higher-pitched, but when Kelly was told he sounded rather like a chipmunk he decided to draw out the pathos and turn the song into a slow lament.

That underlines the power the Stereophonics now wielded over their audience. They could now demand their fans' full and undiverted attention, as Stuart realised. 'When we started,' he recalled, 'we just wanted to get into people's faces, and the only way we knew of doing that was with loud songs.' Now, he reasoned with a wink, 'it's not so small-town... there's less songs about trees.'

The idea for 'Plastic California' had come to Kelly in the back of a hearse, of all places! Their long-time idol Neil Young used to drive a coffin-carrier with his earliest band's gear in the back, but this particular big black car was used for a macabre trip around Los Angeles visiting the houses and last resting places of dead film stars. It says lots about the American sense of entertainment that such a tour exists... and just as much about the Stereophonics' macabre curiosity for taking the trip!

'It's not really life on the road, it's experience on the road... taken from experiences on our travels.'

Insistent, relentless yet chimingly melodic underneath a forbidding exterior, 'Plastic California' was a song *Rock Sound* reviewer Nick Smith termed 'slightly eerie and panoramic, reminiscent of Screaming Trees, with hints of AC/DC, the Kinks and Buffalo Tom.' Its subject matter and inspiration, like 'Pick A Part That's New', reflected how far the boys' worldview had broadened since their first efforts; as Kelly put it, *Performance And Cocktails* was 'an album that asks a lot of questions. We've been chucked into a lot of situations we've had to learn to deal with, and we've probably seen ten years of experiences in the span of two. You just ask what is all that about, and it doesn't answer a lot of questions it just asks a lot. It's not really life on the road, it's experience on the road... taken from experiences on our travels. It's not the Scorpions or Ted Nugent.' Indeed...

So how to finish an album like this? 'I Stopped To Fill My Car Up', a song totally without guitars, was the unexpected answer. It could have fallen flat on its face but didn't. Lyrical inspiration came from another 'story a bloke told me', about stopping for petrol late one night and a stranger just climbing into the back of his car. Just who *was* the man with 'a bag full of money'? We have to decide for ourselves... but he could have been a Bartender! That song came to Kelly next morning in what was clearly a very fertile period.

Musically, '...Fill My Car Up' would never have come together without the gift of a piano, which came into the Jones household in April

1998 thanks to his long-time girlfriend Emma, with whom he'd just moved in. 'She works in a hairdresser's and this woman wanted to give us a piano... we swopped it for a Stereophonics T-shirt.' A fair exchange which gave us this classic, composed when Kelly came back from the cinema late one night. Since he claims the only song he's proficient enough to play on the keyboard is John Lennon's masterpiece 'Imagine', it's unlikely he'll be throwing out the guitar *just* yet – but this ballad is, as he says, 'perfect to finish the album.'

The final touch was added by backing vocalist Astrid to a track *Q* magazine would hail as its standout. 'At its end, *Performance And Cocktails* pulls off a masterstroke with 'I Stopped To Fill My Car Up'. A fabulous song which moves along a ghostly piano line, it sounds as odd and inspired as Bruce Springsteen fronting Pink Floyd. If this is the future of the Stereophonics, the best is certainly yet to come.'

'I'd like to class the Stereophonics as a Premier League band, and by the release of this second album they will be.'

For Richard, the whole thing had been an intensely pleasurable experience. 'This album shows different sides to the band, the harder-edged stuff and the tender ballads. We'd had a lot of experience in the studio from the first album, so this one was, if anything, easier.' He also praised V2 for not interfering with the creative process. 'They leave us to get on with what we're doing, but we do listen to them when it comes to singles. They're pretty much pop songs, but for this album as a whole we've gone the more mature way.'

The album had taken shape in no fewer than six recording studios – Courtyard, Parkgate, RealWorld, Woolhall, Eden and Rockfield. It was produced, like its predecessor, by the Bird and Bush team, Marshall Bird also being credited with Hammond organ, Fender Rhodes electric keyboard, acoustic piano and Mellotron (an old-fashioned string synthesiser popular in the 1960s like the one the Beatles used on 'Strawberry Fields Forever').

V2's Dave Wibberley was understandably enthusiastic about the new songs. 'Like a diary, Kelly writes about what he's experiencing at the time, and the new lyrics are just as graphic about being under pressure as the band's suddenly in the spotlight.' His colleague David Steele had high hopes, too. 'I'd like to class the Stereophonics as a Premier League band, and by the release of this second album they will be.'

'I think we've grown up as a band,' explained Kelly. 'It sounds a lot looser, a lot scruffier and not so organised, but then again it sounds a lot better as well. I think touring a lot has turned us into better musicians, and that comes across a lot better on tape.' Mixmaster Al Clay, take a bow…

Kelly admitted before the album came out that he'd been worried if Stereophonics fans would take to the shift in direction and emphasis it represented. 'You can play the new stuff and think it's going to piss all over the first album… but then you play a song some nights, look at the people's response and wonder if they're going to get the new stuff in the same way.' He needn't have worried.

Press reaction to the album was generally positive, though the band's rapid rise in status had clearly also upped expectations a good deal. *Q* magazine's Paul Rees, the man who'd waxed lyrical about track 13, disappointingly gave the whole creation just three stars out of five, dubbing this 'a good album, but not a great one.' He singled out some fine songs like 'the two stately ballads, 'Is Yesterday Tomorrow Today?' and 'A Minute Longer', plus 'She Takes Her Clothes Off',' and praised the 'welcome degree of restraint to be found on 'Hurry Up And Wait' and 'Just Looking'.' But, all things considered, he felt the album was 'at least three tracks too long' and that the Stereophonics 'remain a comfortable, familiar band rather than an exciting one.'

Select's Roy Wilkinson also came up with a distinctly average three out of five verdict. While most underwhelmed critics would slate the Phonics for being samey, he claimed perversely that, in the end, '*Performance And Cocktails* doesn't rock quite enough.' *Rock Sound* magazine's Nick Smith was more satisfied, a four stars out of five review reflecting this.

"The album crashes in with 'Roll Up And Shine', a taut, edgy monster powered by Stuart's powerhouse drumming and Kelly's vocals sounding even more raw, throaty and downright sexy than before. Then it's straight into the insanely catchy three-minute blast of the hit single "The Bartender And The Thief", which is further proof of Kelly's storytelling genius.' And so on…

This time round, 'serious' broadsheets like the *Guardian* gave the album plenty of column inches, that paper's reviewer praising the uptempo numbers like 'The Bartender And The Thief', 'Roll Up And Shine' and 'Just Looking' as 'effortlessly catchy, Jones rasping like a chainsaw slicing through oak.'

It was back on the bus in April for the *Performance And Cocktails* UK Tour, with all roads leading to Morfa. They'd play a total of 17 shows to a total of 39,407 people, kicking off with two sold-out shows at Glasgow Barrowlands in mid-month and ending at Brixton Academy on 2 May. This latter was notable for the fact that *Melody Maker* committed heresy and printed a slag-off review – possibly their first ever. Entitled 'A Thousand ZZZs', as in snores, it suggested that the Stereophonics were 'simple, old-fashioned and unspecial.' A selection of audience members interviewed as a sidebar to the piece interestingly begged to differ. Backlash? What backlash?

Having accomplished their tour successfully (in everyone's eyes but that *Melody Maker* reviewer, anyway), the band were in prime form to play the Toxic Twin Towers Ball, T in the Park – which they co-headlined, Kelly unusually smashing one of his guitars on stage – and a warm-up gig at Liverpool's Royal Court four days before the gig to end them all.

The single to send them on their way rejoicing was 'Pick A Part That's New'. Rather than reflect the feeling of New York *ennui* that inspired the song, the trio decided to take another tack entirely and use the video to pay homage to Michael Caine's classic 1960s movie *The Italian Job*. 'We had a right old laugh, as you can see from our grins,' confirmed Kelly of what was their most enjoyable video shoot so far in Italy back in February, zipping around the place in Mini Coppers.

This was a number *Q* magazine had described as 'a jaunty song, with much use of acoustic guitars and singer Kelly Jones resisting the temptation to bellow each line as if his head were exploding.' As ever with Stereophonics singles, those who invested in the format would find more for their money that they'd bargained for. The B-sides on this occasion included covers of a couple of American classics. 'Something In The Way' was originally cut by another well-known and liked three-piece band, Nirvana, while 'Positively Fourth Street' came from the pen of one Robert Zimmerman, alias Bob Dylan, who released the song way back in 1965 and whose equally rollicking 'Subterranean Homesick Blues' had been the regular encore number of the Tragic Love Company all those years ago.

These two fascinating choices were joined, depending on which format you bought, by a new Phonics song, 'Nice To Be Out', or an acoustic version of 'Pick A Part...' accompanied by the video in computer-compatible form. The song gave the band their second successive Number 4 hit, peaking on its entry date of 15 May behind a gruesome trio of boy bands – Boyzone, Westlife and 911. They'd already achieved a Top 3 place, of course, with 'The Bartender And The Thief' in late '98, so the disappointment could have been worse.

As far as the album went, though, things could hardly have gone better. It entered the UK charts on 20 March at the very top, displacing all-fiddling Irish darlings the Corrs, and would go on to sell 600,000 copies in its first four months of issue, stay 16 weeks in the Top 10 and be nominated for the prestigious Mercury Music Prize (whose previous winners had included Pulp, Gomez and Roni Size).

As Richard explained, it was all part of the masterplan. 'Everything has grown from last year, winning the Brit Award, then all the singles climbing steadily up the charts and now the album going straight in at Number 1. Our plan early on was to have a gradual progression, and that's pretty much what has happened.' (It's said that, on the week of release, *Performance And Cocktails* was outselling Robbie Williams' second effort by a factor of two to one.)

Not that all this had been achieved without effort, both in the studio, on stage and behind the scenes with their record company. Having been the V2 label's first signing, the Stereophonics were now quite clearly both their biggest band and brightest hopes – and, recognising this, the company had rolled a major publicity machine into action to promote the release. This included a TV ad campaign which would win the band further fame in quite an unexpected (but highly amusing) way.

The ad was voiced by the inimitable Kathy Burke, alias Waynetta Slob of *Harry Enfield Show* fame and a confirmed Phonics fan. Her catchline for the commercial – 'get off your arse and buy it' – used a four-letter word that most of us would consider mild in terms of late-1990s standards but one which caused all of two viewers to get off their... er, behinds and complain to the Independent Television Commission. They, in turn, ruled that the word was inappropriate to be used on a TV commercial, having carried out market research that claimed to prove that around a third of the viewing public considered 'arse' a 'severe' or 'very severe' word to be used on the telly.

Kelly could barely conceal his mirth, revealing that Kathy had done two different versions of the ad to be used before and after the 9.00pm watershed when all impressionable children are supposed to vanish upstairs or turn into pumpkins. 'I think if she'd had her way,' he concluded, 'she'd have gone a lot further and said "Fucking buy it." She's *great!*'

The Phonics paid her back by donating 'Just Looking' as the opening music to her film, *This Year's Love*, which came out in February and also starred Ian Hart (who played John Lennon in the Beatles film *Backbeat*). The soundtrack album for the film, which Kelly described as 'a cross between *Four Weddings And A Funeral* and *Trainspotting*,' came out on V2 and also featured the likes of Garbage, Travis and Ocean Colour Scene.

Kathy had been at the Stereophonics' first major TV appearance on *Later With Jools Holland*, and ever since had declared herself a committed fan of this 'brilliant band'. For their part, the Phonics thought the song perfectly encapsulated the film's plot-line. 'It's a really good film, a lot of British actors will do very well out of it. Kathy is brilliant, I think she just played herself. It's good the way the characters intertwine. It's pretty much exactly what the song is: different types of lifestyles, different relationships, expectations of relationships, stuff like that... always waiting for something better to come along, which never happens.'

'I nearly had a heart attack, I felt like I was watching myself from afar... I was in a daze all day.'

Something very good that came along in the summer of 1999 was an invitation to one of the rock calendar's major events – and one scheduled for the third anniversary of the Stereophonics' signing of their record deal. As its title implied, the Toxic Twin Towers Ball was a party hosted by American rock legends Aerosmith. They'd had to cancel previous British dates due to illness within the band, and once back on the road had promised their fans the ultimate in concert experiences.

The result was a gig at Wembley, whose Twin Towers were shortly to go under the demolition man's bulldozer in the same was as Morfa's scheduled redevelopment. Before that, however, a bill was set up to shake the foundations, the Stereophonics looking up at the likes of the Black Crowes and Lenny Kravitz. All this conspired to reduce fast-rising rock star

Kelly Jones to the status of a fan once again. This was a show he'd have happily paid to see...

'I nearly had a heart attack, I felt like I was watching myself from afar... I was in a daze all day. We used to do cover versions of the Black Crowes, Lenny Kravitz and Aerosmith – and there we were on the same stage at Wembley playing with them! I didn't speak to anyone from Aerosmith but they were watching us from the side of the stage – and that was enough to make my legs go. I don't know what I'm doing here... everything's gone a bit strange.'

Backstage with Howard Marks

With video cameras shadowing his every move and Richard and Stuart many metres away across a stage the size of a tennis court, a black-clad Kelly felt this was light years away from the impromptu rugby singalong at the same venue six months or so before. It wasn't until he advanced to the front of the apron, where Steve Tyler would later be prancing in camply Jagger-esque style, and saw a pal from Cwmaman atop another mate's shoulders and weaving at him, that he regained his grip on reality.

It wasn't just any old mate, either… but the *other* Richard Jones, who'd once augmented them on guitar. Had things been different, he could have been sharing the stage with them rather than applauding wildly from the mosh pit. 'My girlfriend cuts his hair,' Kelly recalls thinking… Real life was back again and from then on, somehow, it was plain sailing.

Many family members and friends managed to get backstage to lig at the biggest heavy rock event of the summer, rubbing shoulders with world-famous names they'd only ever read about in the pages of *Kerrang!* Richard remained inscrutable behind his shades no matter who he was being pictured with, but Stuart's smile was so wide as to make floodlights unnecessary. The highlight of the whole shebang for Kelly's aunt was running into Steven Tyler – literally! Her gasp of 'It can't be…' was met by a cheery 'You'd better believe it, baby!'

There was an unpublicised flip side to the Wembley show on the following day when performers played to an invited audience – including shock-rocker Alice Cooper – to raise money for two worthy causes, ABC (Action for Brazil's Children) and SCREAM (Supporting Children through Re-education And Music). Venue was the posh Café de Paris, in London's Leicester Square.

By this time, the Stereophonics could have been forgiven about being a touch blasé – but press attention was elsewhere this time, as former Wimbledon tennis champion turned rock'n'roller Pat Cash (in town as an Australian TV commentator) teamed up with Queen's Roger Taylor. In even bigger news, Jimmy Page joined forces with the Robinson brothers from Black Crowes and the Toxic Twins themselves, Joe Perry and Steven Tyler, to riff their way through some well-known rock songs and Led Zep classics. All these musicians signed a guitar to be auctioned for the charities concerned.

But the Stereophonics had a surprise up their sleeves too in the shape of Billy Duffy, blond bombshell guitarist with 1980s new wave/metal band the Cult. Kelly, Richard and Stuart had been sauntering down a street in Camden *en route* for the Café de Paris when Duffy emerged from a restaurant and literally bumped into them. Their paths having crossed before, he asked if they were playing the gig and, if so, whether they'd be up for a collaboration.

'He said (singer) Ian Astbury might be coming along,' Kelly later elaborated, 'because the Cult are getting back together, but then it came to the night and he didn't show up. But we did the song anyway.' The collaborators apparently rehearsed the song, 'Wild Flower', backstage 'playing air guitars', and it topped off a short, 25-minute set that comprised 'The Bartender And The Thief', 'Pick A Part That's New', 'Hurry Up And Wait', 'Too Many Sandwiches' and 'Check My Eyelids For Holes'.

The charity gig was a curious concept, with champagne being freely dispensed and exotic foods scoffed in apparent disregard for the poverty of those the event was supposed to be helping. Kelly was all too aware of the dichotomy, which seemed to bother him a lot more than the fact that few were paying him and his band the attention they deserved. 'This is about a working-class wedding,' was how he chose to introduce 'Too Many Sandwiches', before adding plaintively 'I don't suppose there's anyone still working class in here?'

As the million sales mark for *Performance And Cocktails* came and went in August, it was clear that the Stereophonics were well and truly in the big league. Coming across Liam Gallagher a couple of months earlier when staying in a London hotel, they'd engaged in an impromptu (and doubtless inebriated) version of 'The Bartender And The Thief'. Like every Phonics fan the country long, Liam was word-perfect, and once news of the bar-room performance spread the tabloid hunt was on for pictures of Kelly and Liam together.

Gallagher's band, Oasis, may have recorded a song called 'The Masterplan', but the Stereophonics were living the dream. Few of Richard Branson's blueprints had come off in quite as spectacular a fashion; the boys from Cwmaman could have been excused for drinking his health.

chapter 9:

THE FUTURE

The success of Morfa posed a question: where to go after the biggest gig of your life? 'The New Millennium Stadium' (Kelly) and 'The Moon' (Stuart) were two offbeat possibilities. More down to earth was a tour of Wales's rugby grounds – a venture that would, said Kelly, redress an imbalance. 'We haven't really done any work in the north apart from the Snowdonia benefit, so I think it's time we went up there'.

Yet though everything in the Stereophonics garden seemed rosy enough, the perceptive view of *New Musical Express* scribe Stuart Bailie in his account of the events of 31 July had injected a note of caution that none of the rave reviews elsewhere had shared. 'Kelly Jones,' he observed, 'writes his songs from the viewpoint of an outsider, who's dismayed at the rituals of drinking, shagging, toiling and dying. His vision is basically bleak, allied to the underdog, yet tonight he's telling his stories to a bullish crowd who are cheerfully punching the air and getting it on.'

Bailie's conclusion pulled no punches. 'Those little-town blues are effectively dissipating, leaving Kelly Jones in a tricky place between consensus and dissent. between the instinct to find approval and the contrary urge to go view society from its edge. There's a lot to hold out for. Hopefully he won't be welshing on the deal ahead.' The headline of the piece? 'Kelly, Watch The Stardom…'

Certainly, America was a country where they expected their rock stars to be larger than life. And the States would be the Stereophonics' next stop, with a series of shows scheduled for October. They'd be renewing acquaintances with the Black Crowes, while the other group in the package would be Live, a band whose radio-friendly albums in the Stereophonics' mould had attracted critical praise over there if not yet in Britain. *The Guardian* believed the Welsh wonders had every chance of Stateside success. 'There's something going on here, and I suspect Phonicsmania will spread, even to America, where currently a Welsh band would have trouble getting arrested.'

The tour would serve to boost the 14 September release of *Performance And Cocktails*, and hopes were high for a *Billboard* chart showing. It would be heralded by 'Pick A Part That's New', whose release to radio came three weeks beforehand. No-one doubted it would take work to crack this important new market, given that the trio's previous tour behind *Word Gets Around* had only managed to push national sales to the 8,000 mark. 'I must admit I thought the last record would fly on something like KROQ,' said Kelly, referring to a famous Los Angeles radio station, 'but we'll put in the effort (for *Performance...*) if the record company will.'

And there was little doubt of that, as V2's American product manager Sharon Lord outlined to trade paper *Billboard*. 'There's plenty for us to talk about. We've started with a lot of Internet promotion, and we're also starting some grass-roots marketing, with flyers and CD samplers. We'll have them over before the release date to do at least showcases in New York, possibly also Los Angeles, then we'll have them back in October and November.'

The American media had been flown over *en masse* to witness Morfa, and their impressions must surely have been favourable. And that certainly was the case in late August when the Stereophonics played yet more festivals in Britain and Europe. Yet the peculiar thing was that they were very definitely not bill-toppers in any of the cases. The two-day, two-venue V99 event at Chelmsford and Staffordshire saw them down-bill to Suede, whose latest album *Head Music* had entered the chart at Number 1 in May, deposing Abba, only to head downwards like a brick. Conversely, Blur were the band in bigger letters when the bands headed over to Europe in a communal private jet.

'I've got no problem with Blur,' said Kelly, making the point that their hit album *Parklife*, released at the height of Brit-pop mania in 1994, 'has probably sold more than the rest of us put together, so let's not get above ourselves.' As for Brett Anderson's mob, he felt it was too soon for the Stereophonics to top the bill over a band with that big a back catalogue. 'I don't want to be in that position yet.' The yet that ends that statement is crucial...

The Chelmsford leg of V99, where Kelly wore a large, black, Afro-style wig for a bet, saw their Sunday set once again acclaimed by *Kerrang!* as 'sheer brilliance'. Interestingly, the Manic Street Preachers had headlined the Saturday bill, and were castigated in the self-same review as having produced 'a performance of rare mediocrity'. The Manics, said unpitying pundit Ian Fortnam, were 'teetering on the brink of becoming an entirely spent force... sleepwalking on what seems like automatic pilot.'

The Stereophonics, on the other hand, gave a show that 'only serves to accentuate the tragic ongoing demise of the Manics... (by) the easy interaction between band and audience, the obvious enjoyment they take from their performance... As 'Local Boy In The Photograph' unites every set of lungs in Chelmsford, the Stereophonics swallow V99 whole.' It was apparent, though, that having introduced new songs into their act some while ago, the Phonics would have to inject further fresh material sometime soon to avoid accusations of playing the same set too often.

In retrospect, the timing of *Performance And Cocktails* to break through just couldn't have been better. Oasis had decided to take a year off, Suede were conspicuous by their absence, Pulp were quiet and Blur were busy reinventing themselves and shearing thousands off their sales figures as they did so. And, as reviews like Chelmsford suggested, the Manics had milked their albums for every possible single, and were teetering on the edge of a backlash.

Films seemed to loom large in the possible scheme of things, the Phonics having impressed the big-screen boys by their amazing videos. Ade Edmondson and Rik Mayall from alternative comedy team *The Young Ones* and *Bottom* had already asked for the band to contribute a new song to a film they were making, while as already mentioned 'Just Looking' had featured as the opening music to *This Year's Love*. As well as being what Kelly laughingly termed 'one of those happy marketing moments' (V2 also doing the soundtrack), it had tied in nicely because of the premise around which the film was built – that you have seven different relationships before you find the person you truly love.

To further cement their links to the unreal world of cinema, Kelly had been headhunted to play the lead in a forthcoming film musical by leading director Baz Luhrmann, whose CV included *Romeo And Juliet, Strictly Ballroom* and, ironically, the summer 1999 novelty hit single 'Everybody's Free To Wear Sunscreen'. He made his enquiry towards the start of the year, and Kelly admitted he had been daunted as well as flattered by the offer. 'A movie would be an odd thing to do. It's a hell of a thing to start getting yourself into,' he stated, adding he'd never acted in his life, making the perceptive point that 'not many musicians make good actors.'

As it was, the filming of the musical was scheduled to start in August, when the group would be playing festivals and preparing for their conquest of America. An altogether more important aim, all agreed, than playing the thespian (or the bartender...). His abandonment of film stardom, for the moment anyway, didn't prevent Kelly fronting up at the Cannes Film Festival that spring with a BBC Radio 1 crew in tow to find out his thoughts on the proceedings.

'It's interesting sitting on tables and hearing people pitching scripts to producers,' he revealed, musing on his own scriptwriting ambitions that were curtailed – temporarily at least – with the band's V2 signing. 'It's something I'd love to come back to in the future. I'm in no hurry,' he added swiftly, aware that thousands of fans would be paling at the thought of him hanging up his guitar. 'It's great to experience what I've been experiencing, which will probably give me script ideas for the future, but I'm very happy doing the band at the moment.'

If he was to be a leading light in the Welsh film wave that had started with *Twin Town*, either as a performer or a scriptwriter, it seemed likely he might join forces with Rhys Ifans, most recently seen starring opposite Hugh Grant in *Notting Hill*. 'He's a brilliant actor, and the way he's going he's going to be a big star.' Mind you, it was quite a jump from budding

scriptwriter to Kelly's favoured *alter ego* when booking in at hotels... Billy Shakespeare!

Stuart would remember 1999 as the year he took the plunge and became the first Phonic to tie the knot. He spent his stag night in the less than glamorous surroundings of Poole, Dorset, having hired a minibus to take his pals down from Cwmaman. In the end, he and the others took a roundabout route, as they'd been booked to play *TFI Friday*. 'By the time we got to Poole everyone was absolutely *steaming*,' he later recalled through an alcoholic haze. 'We were just trying to catch up for the next three hours.'

This was to prove, in fact, just the first of three pre-nuptial bevies that Stuart would preside over. The second and third took place closer to home, one in a club, the second a 'quiet drink' the night before, and both were 'really mental'. He reckoned around 1,200 friends in total took part in sending him down the aisle: 'One of my mates said that two years ago I wouldn't have been able to fill a phone box.'

The lucky lady to whom Stuart pledged his troth was Nicola, a university-educated occupational therapist whose chosen career couldn't have been further from the rock'n'roll world inhabited by her new hubby. 'She deals with terminally ill patients, stroke victims, kids,' says Cable, crediting the love of his life with helping put his own existence into perspective. Instead of discussing his hobnobbing with Jimmy Page, 'we talk about some old woman who's maybe been married for 75 years and now her husband's at death's door and she's going to be left on her own...' For relaxation, the couple shared a common pastime – golf. Well, if it's good enough for Alice Cooper...

Kelly, for his part, was finding it hard to reconcile his life and his relationship quite as easily, revealing to *Q* magazine that he'd spent some time away from home in the late spring of 1999. Three months of promotional work had, it seemed, taken its toll and he needed his own space. 'We're back together now,' he said of himself and long-time girlfriend Emma, 'but my head went a bit pear-shaped. She's completely cool... I said I needed a few days and the few days turned into two months. We've been best mates a long time. And I'm not ideal for her at all, really.'

Kelly had returned from French leave in Cannes to discover that a benefit show for war-torn Kosovo was to be held at the Forum in north London. Having immediately volunteered the band's services via a phonecall to Oasis's Noel Gallagher, one of the venture's leading lights, he discovered the bonus that Paul Weller would be there. From that, it was a short step to proposing a collaboration on 'Traffic', which the former Jam mainman stated he was very much looking forward to. 'It's nice to see different generations of musicians up there all 'avin' it,' said the Modfather. 'I don't know many of the new bands, I'm no authority on the new music, but I'm behind them because I think they're a good band.'

Kelly, who admitted he'd listened to Weller's Jam recordings with reverence as a kid, was equally delighted to be playing with an even older elder statesman of British rock at the Forum. 'We'll be doing 'Sunny Afternoon' with Ray Davies,' he explained, adding that the experience of doing a soundcheck with Stereophonics' two esteemed collaborators was 'a bit surreal. I'm like a big kid at the moment, so when Noel Gallagher comes in I'll probably fall over.' The band had been playing pubs just along the street three years earlier, and there was no doubting they'd come a long way since then.

Ray Davies, who hailed from nearby Hornsey, had the credentials to be rather more of an 'authority on the new music' than Paul Weller, despite being a decade and a half older. After all, this was the guy who lived with Pretender-in-chief Chrissie Hynde and, more recently, 'kidnapped' Reef's drummer to accompany him on a solo set at one of the festival bills they'd shared. He was more than happy to endorse the Stereophonics as 'nice Welsh lads. I love interacting with the other bands, we'll see how we get on. It's nice for the music to be seen as a collaborative thing rather than a competition. I love the album artwork, and I understand they do one of my songs on stage. There's room for everything, I think they're an interesting band.'

Aside from Weller and Davies, the band's list of famous fans was growing daily. Formula One racing driver Damon Hill and England football captain Alan Shearer had taken in gigs in Dublin and Newcastle respectively, while other artists to claim their services included Robbie Williams and Tom Jones. They'd been due to link with Williams to record a cover version of Adam and the Ants' 1980s hit single 'Antmusic' for the

Disney animated feature film *A Bug's Life*, but the collaborative version never saw the light of day.

A link with fellow Welshman Tom Jones proved more fruitful through. They'd met him just before Christmas 1998, and as a result his son (and manager Mark) reported that, when he flew to Los Angeles to spend Yuletide with the great man, his dad was lying by the swimming pool listening to their music! Once they'd been convinced this wasn't a wind-up ('if someone had told us that three years ago, we'd have said they were liars'), the boys happily agreed to collaborate on his forthcoming album... which, ironically, also included Robbie Williams!

The Stereophonics weren't the only Welsh connection on the album, since Manic mainman James Dean Bradfield and Catatonia's Cerys Matthews had both been persuaded to participate. Jimmy Dean had been chosen to duet on an Elvis Presley rock classic, 'I'm Left You're Right She's Gone', which one reviewer cruelly summed up as 'Dull youth berated by jolly uncle!' Ms Matthews' participation wasn't surprising, since she'd already guested on Space's hit 'The Ballad Of Tom Jones' with its memorable 'knicker-throwing' lyric. Her link with Jones Senior for a sexy version of the Ray Charles/Betty Carter jazz standard 'Baby It's Cold Outside' would undoubtedly please Kelly's dad, Oscar, and was already being talked about as the last Christmas Number 1 of the millennium.

With all that to live up to, Kelly entered a West London recording studio with Tom in late March 1999 to record the track, a version of Three Dog Night's 1970 US chart-topper 'Mama Told Me (Not To Come)'. He certainly acquitted himself honourably on the Randy Newman-penned number, earning an unexpected round of applause as the microphones were shut off. 'Uncle' Tom related his feelings to a journalist later, calling Kelly 'a local lad from back home, same sense of humour.' As for Mr Bradfield, the same spark clearly hadn't applied. 'A very quiet fellow, but still Welsh... which is important.' 'Reload' was released for the Christmas market late in 1999, and Kelly's contribution was rated as sounding like 'a Valley pub brawl.' A compliment of a sort, we guess...

Ironically, 'Sunny Afternoon', the Kinks song that had made its way into the Phonics' set, had been allocated not to Kelly but Space's Tommy Scott. While the soft-voiced Scouse scally couldn't match our Jones in the pipes department, the elder Jones certainly put real feeling into the line 'the taxman's taken all my dough,' explaining: 'It's a bit like my life story, as I was forced out of Britain in 1974 by the taxman.'

'It was like singing on a Saturday night. In fact, after we'd finished recording the producer came up to me and said "Why don't you sing like that all the time?"'

Yet it was Kelly's performance, likened by some reviewers to Rod Stewart at his peak, that had spurred Tom to his best vocal of the album. 'We had a great time,' said the Stereophonics' hunkiest fan. 'It was like singing on a Saturday night. Kelly's father is a singer, so we know a lot of people in common. And Kelly really goes for it. In fact, after we'd finished recording the producer came up to me and said "Why don't you sing like that *all* the time?"'

At the end of the day, Tom Jones provided the lads with a role model as to how to wear their stardom lightly. 'Some people would like us to turn into arrogant rock stars,' explains Kelly, 'but you see someone like him, and he still sounds like a boy from Pontypridd, even though he lives in Los Angeles. It makes you think that you don't *have* to turn into an arsehole.'

Another star invitation that was extended to them around this time was to participate in a tribute album for Ian Dury, the Cockney 'Rhythm Stick' hitmaker of the late 1970s who was suffering from cancer. This would have been avidly taken up by Kelly, who admired the man's witty lyrics, but by the time they were able to explore the possibility all the songs they knew had been claimed.

If it's August it must be the *Kerrang!* Awards. This time round, the Stereophonics were up for six – Best British Live Act, Best Single ('Just Looking'), Best Album (*Performance And Cocktails*), Best Video

('Pick A Part That's New'), Best British Band and Best Band In The World. In the event, they were more than happy to double last year's haul and pick up Best British Band and Best Album.

For fans of retro TV and movies, it was undoubtedly a thrill to be presented with the latter gongs by Detective Ken Hutchinson from the hit 1970s cop show *Starsky And Hutch*. Blond actor David Soul who, since his crimebusting stint, had been a singing star of the saccharine ballad variety. Come to that (and there were probably few heavy-metal critics present who'd have known) he'd gone further that the Phonics themselves by topping the UK chart in early 1977. Would 'Don't Give Up On Us Baby' join 'Sunny Afternoon' as a rare cover in the Stereophonic repertoire? Only time would tell... but Stuart was heard giving his all on another 'Soulful' hit, 'Silver Lady', as the red wine kicked in.

In all seriousness, the acts they beat to take the album Krown (sic) included the Red Hot Chili Peppers (*Californication*) and Marilyn Manson (*Mechanical Animals*), not to mention heavy-metal favourites System of a Down and Silverchair. To those names in the 'World' category could be added Metallica. Stuart rightly claimed their success was 'a tribute to *Kerrang!* readers that we've been allowed to cross over into different categories.'

The Best British Band award was given to them by a well-known and outstanding fan of the band, Melinda Messenger. 'It's always British when you win and Welsh when you lose, innit?' quipped Kelly, who later said that, had they won the Best Live Band category, 'we'd have given it to the Crocketts. No disrespect to the band that won Best Newcomer (Cay), but I thought the Crocketts should have won it. So it would have been nice to give them one of ours...' For Melinda, the evening was a great success 'because I presented an award to my favourite ever band. They're all lovely because they're Welsh, just like my fella.'

The following week's mag had Kelly gazing out from the front cover in big-name company indeed. Jimmy Page, who'd accepted a Hall of Fame award, took centre frame, with crop-headed bassist Shavo Odadjian from System of a Down to the right. And there lay something of a potential problem, because whichever way you looked at it , and however rose-tinted your glasses, Kelly Jones was now the 'face of the Stereophonics'. What this might lead to in the future was anyone's guess...

Most classic rock bands have a figurehead and a lieutenant; Page was perceived as Robert Plant's right-hand man in Led Zeppelin even though he had initially formed the band (as the New Yardbirds) and did a large share of the songwriting. In time, both came to be known as symbols of that respected band. Likewise, Ozzy Osbourne and Tony Iommi have become joint figureheads of Black Sabbath. Even though the Double O stood out front in unique style, anyone with more than a passing interest identified the saturnine Sabs guitarist, standing in the shadows side-stage, as the power behind the loon.

What could be 'in it' for Kelly going solo in the future? Well, the democratic song credits, showing all three members as writing the music, were a positive side of a band determined to show they were more than the sum of their parts. Yet Kelly alone was credited with the lyrics, revealing that whatever musical arrangements the other two might throw into the pot the small-town inspirations were solely his. Maybe the nearest analogy was Paul Weller, even though the Jam main man had preferred to allow bassist Bruce Foxton the occasional song on an album. He took his three-piece, guitar/bass/drums group as far as he could before running out of steam and opting for a lusher musical pasture in the shape of the keyboard-based Style Council.

Like the Jam, the Stereophonics had come together in a locality, enjoying the status of a street gang and increasing their following on the basis of a hard-gigging itinerary, songs that crossed over to the pop chart and albums that reeked of integrity. In short, the band it was okay for anyone to like. There'd never been another band of that kind until the Stereophonics came along. The Jam existed from 1973 to 1982 – ten years. Depending on where you counted from, the Stereophonics were about to celebrate their tenth birthday (though only the last three had been as a signed band). Only time would tell how many more years they'd enjoy.

'You can do the cliché rock star thing, or you can try and write good songs your whole career and gain respect.'

In many ways, a dispassionate observer would wish them a short, sweet and spectacular life. Because with such a basic line-up the possibilities are necessarily limited, and the only option at the end of the day would be to augment with keyboards, strings, choirs and the kitchen sink. The 'Unplugged' option pursued by Nirvana was already very much a thread in the Phonics' musical tapestry, so there seemed little likelihood that would be much of a change.

Indeed, the trend was to march further down the rock road. So powerful were the musical punches on *Performance*… compared with its predecessor that it almost seemed the spaces between tracks had been shortened, so relentless seemed the songs in their intensity. When it came to words, things were changing too… Given the fact that Kelly considered

Performance And Cocktails reflected seeing 'a lot of different countries over the last two years, and the confusion of seeing so many things in a short space of time,' it seemed likely there'd be a new twist for album number three, whenever it emerged. 'Where we're going lyrically I dunno,' Kelly confessed,' but I don't think it's going to be small-town Cwmaman, because we're not there much any more.'

It is always possible that Richard and Stuart will seek more of a say in the musical direction. Richard, for instance, had found acts like Massive Attack and the Chemical Brothers very much to his liking, and had mischievously messed about with dance-style basslines at soundchecks 'because it's a good way to piss people off... playing like the Chemical Brothers and trying to get the drummer to follow you.' That said, he was always aware that his role was 'not to do anything clumsy or show off.' But if new influences emerged they could either diversify the band's music... or, by causing differences of opinion between members, deal it a potentially mortal blow.

Kelly had certain specific role models in mind when he considered his and the band's future. He divides musicians into two types, the Iggy Pop on one hand and Bob Dylan and Neil Young on the other. 'You can do the cliché rock star thing, or you can try and write good songs your whole career and gain respect.' For him, Dylan was still writing great songs: 'I know which road I'd rather go down...'

Maybe the answer was just to keep on keeping on... as Zeppelin and Sabbath had through the years. The fact that Page was standing at the *Kerrang!* awards at the age of 55 was testament to the fact that great rock can last forever. Sabbath, who were voted Artist of the Millennium, subtly took the piss out of their vintage by sending the younger generation – daughters Toni-Marie Iommi, Aimée Osbourne and 'Biff' Butler, son of Geezer – to pick up the awards in their fathers' steads.

The Sabs' absence might equally have had something to do with the band's touring commitments in the States (which had brought much flak from fans when a projected 'Ozzfest' was cancelled). But, as Kelly recalled, the Stereophonics had interrupted recording of *Performance And Cocktails* to attend the last awards, showing their commitment. 'A lot's happened since then,' he noted, adding that 'I think we're going to get really drunk – this is the first time we've been able to have a drink together without working in ages. It's a boy's night out tonight.'

The *Kerrang!* awards had made it a memorable week, since the Stereophonics had been fulfilling their V99 commitments at Chelmsford and Staffordshire to the usual press rapture. 'They belong utterly in the present,' gushed *Maker* reviewer Robin Bresnark, comparing them favourably with re-formed Manc baggies the Happy Mondays who preceded them on the main stage. 'You just have to wonder whether they can push what they're pushing much further in the future. Still, bugger that, today's set is as blinding as acid-coated contact lenses.' Bresnark concluded that they'd surpassed themselves, 'exuding more confidence that anyone expected and turning everything up another notch just when everyone thought they'd hit their peak.'

If the Stereophonics had become a little blasé about rubbing shoulders with rock aristocracy, an invitation received in the late summer showed again exactly how far they'd come. They were asked to play Wembley Stadium on 9 October as part of an globally televised and staged event billed as 'Live Aid 14 years on'. Net Aid was to take place in Geneva and New York as well as Wembley, with the bill stretching from George Michael and David Bowie through the Corrs and Robbie Williams to the Eurythmics and Stereophonics, their common cause to use the power of the Internet to fight world poverty. VH1, MTV and BBC TV and radio were carrying the music to Britain and the States, with other broadcasters taking sound and pictures worldwide. If there was anything that could rival Morfa in this amazing year, then this was perhaps it.

Yet, as ever, the band felt the need to refresh themselves and touch base with their roots – which they duly did on 24 August by playing to an audience of 400 in London's Sound Republic venue in Leicester Square. Indie radio station XFM were there to take the results to the capital's listeners who were treated to a six-song set: 'Hurry Up And Wait', 'Pick A Part That's New', 'Bartender And The Thief', 'I Wouldn't Believe Your Radio' (the current single, just about to enter the chart at Number 11), 'Just Looking' and 'Local Boy In The Photograph'.

'When you start doing the festivals you forget what the atmosphere at the small clubs was like,' admitted Kelly, who clearly enjoyed the

experience. Next stops on the *Performance And Cocktails* World Tour itinerary would be Australia and, finally, that big push on the States. After that, the next steps for the Stereophonics would be taken on familiar territory – a nine-show arena tour which would take them to eight cities in December and constitute their biggest tour so far in terms of audience numbers.

Starting in Glasgow's SECC on the third, they'd travel north to Aberdeen, crossing the border on their way south to Newcastle before two triumphant nights at Cardiff's International Arena. Then, after a couple of days' rest, the tour picked up again on the 12th at Birmingham's NEC – the venue they'd played as support to James the previous year, Wembley Arena (with the four subsequent nights left empty for possible extra shows), winding up in the steel city of Sheffield for a climactic gig one week before Christmas.

'A lot of our mates back home who have nine to five jobs save all their money so they can go on the piss abroad for two weeks a year, and we get to do it almost every day.'

Then, of course, it would be all back to Cwmaman, where the kids still come knocking for autographs. One lad used to knock on Kelly's door every Sunday without fail. 'I said, "How many have you got now?" He said "23".' Just like the home-town autograph hunter, the Stereophonics showed no sign of losing the thrill of the chase…

Maybe that's because they still remember where they came from. They say some people start performing the moment a light switches on, but for Stuart Cable the illuminating sight of their 'rider' in the dressing room fridge brings home to him time and again just how lucky he is to enjoy his privileged rock-star lifestyle. 'To this day,' he grinds, 'we still look

'This could last ten years or it could last three. And then you're back wrapping cauliflowers.'

at each other when the fridge opens and we see all those cans of Beck's. If our mates were here the fridge'd be fucking empty.' Kelly concurs. 'A lot of our mates back home who have nine to five jobs save all their money so they can go on the piss abroad for two weeks a year, and we get to do it almost every day.'

Richard, the man who lurks behind a microphone on stage but rarely uses it because 'I've got a really bad singing voice', seems to be happy to plough his own furrow. He continues to study Tibetan Buddhism yet insists he's not a practising Buddhist, 'I don't chant, I just read... although it does affect the way you live and think.' On the tour bus, he's known as the Dalai Lama... in joking deference to which he signs the hotel register *Dai* Lama!

His studies have made him mindful of the importance of friendships, not always easy to keep fresh when you're with the other people for such a huge chunk of your life. 'You learn to watch what's happening and act accordingly,' he remarks, adding 'If we'd had a big argument in the band, it could quite easily have ruined it.'

A spiritual dimension hasn't always been an advantage for rock stars; Little Richard was the first to give it all up for God, throwing his rings and trinkets off Sydney Harbour Bridge back in the rock 'n' roll years, while George Harrison and Fleetwood Mac Peter Green were among those to turn their back on fame in search of inner peace. Hopefully, the Stereophonics' bassist could continue to reconcile the rock 'n' roll lifestyle with the needs of his secret soul.

Stuart's view of the long-term future for the Stereophonics is typically upbeat. 'Hopefully we want to stay in this business as long as we can. We always said we're gonna keep on doing this as long as it's fun, and we started this band for the fun reason. And it's great coming across Europe. As long as it's fun we're keeping on.' But let's leave the last word to the man with the insightful pen, Kelly Jones. 'This could last ten years or it could last three. And then you're back wrapping cauliflowers…'

chapter 10:

PERFORM AND EDUCATE

Despite the breath-taking success of *Performance And Cocktails*, it was perhaps understandable that Stereophonics down-to-earth nature would still elicit such quotes as the aforementioned "wrapping cauliflowers" observation. Yet, that smash second album was actually a precursor to far bigger and (musically) far better times ahead. Since the first edition of this book was released in 1999, Stereophonics have graduated to a genuine stadium act, eclipsing even the Morfa triumph and going on to establish themselves as one of the most successful British acts of all time.

The campaign for *Performance And Cocktails* continued unabated with some European dates alongside the Red Hot Chili Peppers and their own aforementioned winter arena tour. Also at this time came the November 1999 release of the two year-old track, 'Hurry Up And Wait'. As previously mentioned, this soft acoustic lilt was a suggestion of Kelly's more subtle writing skills and offered a gentler side to the Stereophonics which an impressed public rewarded by sending it to Number 11. Admittedly, this was not the lofty Top Ten slot which the band were used to by now, but with so many copies of the album having already been sold, it was nonetheless an indicator of the extent of the loyal fan-base the trio had now secured.

The close of 1999 was, of course, drenched in Millennium fever, with all eyes on the over-hyped and over-priced countdown to the new age. Amidst widespread criticism of the commercialisation of the biggest New Year's Eve of all-time, plus public debacles such as the Dome and the 'wobbly' farce of the since-repaired Millennium bridge across the Thames, there was an unfortunate albeit understandable air of cynicism about organised celebrations. Stereophonics chose carefully and agreed to play one of the more credible events, the 31st December headlining billing at Liverpool's Cream.

'Stereophonics have graduated to a genuine stadium act, eclipsing even the Morfa triumph...'

Having already been tipped as one of the hardest working bands in Britain, Stereophonics seemed determined to grasp the crown all for their own by starting the new Millennium with a Stateside tour in February 2000 alongside their British forefathers, Mancunian veterans The Charlatans. Tim Burgess' outfit were a fine example of a band's staying power, having successfully wrenched themselves away from the suffocating shackles of early 90s 'Madchester' and had, like Blur, gone on to establish themselves as an act of genuine substance. This all-British bill represented a tantalising rock double act and, although neither band commanded Billboard-topping followings (yet) in the States, the gigs were met with general critical applause and modest but encouraging sales (a Canadian tour with Our Lady Peace also followed later in the year).

If observers could class the Charlatans as veterans, they were but mere infants compared to the next artist the Stereophonics were to work with - the bona fide legend, Tom Jones. In many ways, the Pontypridd-born

Vegas-conquering icon was a world apart from the earthy image of the Phonics, but in fact the two parties had far more in common than might be immediately obvious. Jones had previously released his aforementioned 1999 album *Reload* - in many ways this was an up-to-date re-working of his hugely successful late 60s television show, *This Is Tom Jones*, a programme whose litany of big-name guests accompanied by Jones's astonishing vocals helped make him one of the few genuine world mega-stars. Later, the so-called 'Boy From Nowhere' dabbled with the alternative music scene on his much-vaunted collaboration with avante garde noise pioneers, The Art Of Noise, but it wasn't until *Reloaded* that a completely new generation discovered the extent of his talent.

It was a measure of Tom's admiration for the Stereophonics' talent that their joint single, 'Mama Told Me (Not To Come)' was chosen for release in late January 2000. With a *Top of the Pops* performance to boost its profile, the track easily reached Number 3. The band's hefty consolidation in 2000 then continued when the *NME* announced that the Morfa concert was their 'Gig of the Year'. This coincided with news that *Performance And Cocktails* was the fifth biggest-selling album of 1999 and had now reached quadruple platinum status in the UK alone, with a total of over two million sales worldwide (even *Word Gets Around* was approaching double platinum status).

Having barely paused for breath since their career started to take off, Stereophonics finally entered a phase where they found themselves in the same country for more than a few weeks! Summer 2000 was scheduled to be left relatively untouched as the window in which they were to record their third album. As always, particularly with Kelly's perfectionism in mind, the band were determined to produce a record they would be proud of. This time there was the added outside pressure of following up a multi-platinum selling predecessor and consolidating their reputation as arguably Britain's biggest band (Travis had come along with their excellent *The Man Who* long player as genuine challengers, but meanwhile Oasis, Blur and other key players remained notably quiet - even the Manic Street Preachers seemed to have lost some of their infamous fire in the belly that had so fuelled their early output).

The band duly headed up the M4 towards the spa town of Bath, where they entrenched themselves for the sessions at Peter Gabriel's world class Real World Studios. Generally the time in Bath was highly productive, although Kelly later admitted to Q magazine that the sessions were not without their tensions: "I was in the studio spending all my time on the new record and neglecting the boys. I was ignoring people because I wanted to get the job done. So Stuart's sitting there for hours waiting for something he can listen to and, in the end, he just fucked off. And I'm like, You lazy cunt. Now I think, You were right to do that." (Stuart reciprocates by saying he feels "guilty" and "should have stuck around.") Elsewhere, Kelly was open about how tiring their gruelling schedules could be: "We'd toured for five years and we felt jaded. We really had to decide whether or not we wanted to do it anymore, and we had to make a record that ensured we'd all be interested in playing."

Kelly was also in the middle of breaking up with his girlfriend whereas Stuart was expecting a son (Cian, born in February 2001) and Richard was about to get married (to Gail, a fashion stylist and designer who didn't mind his growing collection of Harleys!). Kelly admits that he is perhaps the most introspective of the trio (although Stuart is said to be the shyest - and loudest!) Still, the sessions moved along well although they were never as protracted as the dusk til dawn efforts for *Performance And Cocktails*! So, as the summer festivals loomed, the new album was taking shape. Interest in the band was kept suitably high by the re-release of their singles back-catalogue, many of which had become increasingly difficult for the masses of hording fans to get hold of.

Unusually for such a gig-hungry act, Stereophonics only broke the momentum of the recording sessions for three gigs - and it is a sign of just how huge the band had become that these three shows were all enormous - headlining the Reading, Leeds and Glasgow three-site festival in August. If the record-buying public had somehow managed to forget the Stereophonics (difficult when their previous album was still selling thousands), the three festival slots in late August were the perfect reminder. The band enjoyed them too, not least because it felt like they hadn't gigged in Britain for ages. Also, the Reading show was boosted by the guest appearance of Mr Tom Jones himself. Kelly had previously also made a low key appearance on stage with the mighty Paul Weller at the latter's Brixton Academy show in May 2000, for a duet of 'The Woodcutters Son'.

Few snippets about the new record were offered, keeping the millions of fans in suspense, but Stuart did tell BBC Radio 1 that, "I think Kelly gets his inspiration from seeing different parts of the world. There's one (track) on there about a shoeshine guy which is quite funny. It's about this guy just sitting in the airport who started talking to us, a bit of a mad man, and he shines shoes all day... The rockier songs are gonna be more rocky and the slower songs are going to be more acoustic-y."

Fans' appetites were also kept whetted by a collaboration with Cardiff band Manchild. The track was entitled 'The Clichés Are True' and saw a September 2000 release on One Little Indian Records. Kelly penned the lyrics and also played the heavy guitar riffs featured on the track. Manchild had previously enlisted other rockers to augment their breakbeat/metal blend, including the perennially under-rated Andy Cairns of Therapy?, on the band's previous single 'Rehab'.

In October 2000, rumours began to circulate on the web that Kelly was in fact planning to leave the Stereophonics and pursue a solo tour. It transpired that what he actually had planned was a series of low key solo acoustic gigs, designed to showcase the more varied and subtle material on the forthcoming new album. Having headlined in most of the UK's biggest venues and festivals, this was a welcome change in scale for Kelly (and something that the band enjoyed so much that they replicated it with an early 2001 North American tour of a similar acoustic nature).

The eight dates quickly sold-out and kicked off in Dublin on the 13th of November, heading through Brighton, Bath, Glasgow, Edinburgh, York, Birmingham and Cardiff. It was during these gigs that Kelly first aired his cover of the Mike D'Abo song made famous by Rod Stewart, namely, 'Handbags & Gladrags', a future Phonics single.

Despite their huge success, Stuart had opted to stay in his hometown, but first Richard and then Kelly both bought places to live in London. Kelly also bought a new house in Cwmaman too, alongside his flat in trendy Fulham, west London. Aside from the album recording sessions, Kelly was also asked to speak at the Oxford University Union - he declined, saying "I never imagined appealing to that side of the world. I just used to think of people in a pub somewhere sticking our records on a jukebox, like we did with Thin Lizzy." It was also rumoured he'd been invited to audition for the hit Baz Luhrmann film *Moulin Rouge* and even asked to appear naked in *Cosmopolitan*! (yes, he declined that too)

Autumn 2000 was also a good time for adding to the band's list of celebrity acquaintances, most impressively perhaps with an appearance at the Who charity gig at the Royal Albert Hall on 27th November. Kelly was mixing with the legendary Pete Townshend-led band as well as other stars on the night such as Noel Gallacher. He was introduced to Paul McCartney and has since become friends with the Rolling Stones' Ronnie Wood, Keith Richards and World Snooker Champion, Ronnie O'Sullivan amongst others. The band's affinity with the Who was later recognised when they appeared on the spring 2001 tribute album to that band, namely *Substitute - The Songs of the Who*.

'The rockier songs are gonna be more rocky and the slower songs are going to be more acoustic-y!'

The Phonics' contribution was 'Who Are You' as well as a CD Rom featuring Kelly's duo with the Who at the Royal Albert Hall performing 'Substitute'. Other artists on the record included Ocean Colour Scene, Paul Weller, David Bowie, Pearl Jam and Sheryl Crow. Pete Townshend said of the record how "about a year ago, Bobby Pridden, who has worked as our sound man for about 35 years, came and asked me if he could put together a tribute album to The Who. Since then I've left him to it and I'm amazed and flattered at the number of great artists he's managed to involve."

March 2001 saw the Phonics return to the serious stuff - the first single from the forthcoming new album. Entitled 'Mr Writer', the soft, edgy yet strangely infectious riff-led track was a great showcase for Kelly's trademark gravel-ly vocals. It was solemn, grandiose and musically deft. Accompanied by a video featuring the band dressed as very odd, dark circus clowns, the single was a fitting taster for the more sophisticated and mature material soon to be released on the new album. The lead track was backed by two other new tracks, 'Maritim Belle Vue In Kiel' and 'An Audience With Mr Nice', as well as two live acoustic tracks, 'Hurry Up And Wait' and 'Don't Let Me Down' across the various formats. The inspiration for the song was

> **'I think the song's been blown out of proportion. It's just another environment I write about.'**

summed up nicely by this quote from Kelly: "Someone once told me, if a journalist reviews an album after just one or two listens he can only be writing about himself. So make of that what you will."

The barbed track saw the band walk, perhaps not surprisingly, straight into press controversy. Openly critical of the music journalists that the band came into daily contact with, the tirade seemed unexpected considering the group were about to launch a new record which would then be reviewed by these very same people. But it was perhaps this very 'untouchable' nature of these writers that Kelly so objected to. He was happy to qualify his criticism: "They're aching for me to say which journalist it's about. It's not about any one in particular - though I like to keep 'em on their toes." Indeed, he suggested the single was more a sarcastic commentary on the music business in general rather than a personal attack on one individual in particular: "(The industry) has become much more about marketing and celebrity status than it is about music. Some journalists seem only interested in celebrity as well. It's the British weeklies we're talking about. It's not the proper magazines like *Q* or *Mojo*."

Kelly was keen to play down any talk of an impending battle with the music scribes, telling *NME.com* that, "I think the song's been exaggerated and blown out of proportion. It's just another environment I write about. It's not necessarily about any dig or any journalist, we haven't really had that much in the way of bad press. We had a song and I had the title 'Mr Writer' and I just wrote this cynical, dark little story. It's not about personal jibes."

Many music journalists were suitably unconvinced and the record received modest reviews, but this did not prevent it becoming the week's highest new entry on the UK charts at Number 5 on its March 19th release, helped by strong coverage on prime time weekend shows such as the ever-popular *CD:UK*.

The furore surrounding 'Mr Writer' certainly did little to dampen Kelly's willingness to talk to the press. At this time, he also talked energetically about the Napster controversy which had embroiled the internet, namely the legal action taken against that company for alleged copyright infringement by a number of record companies. He said that he felt the downloading of songs was not much different to taping albums as he did when he was young and that the fact fans might know lyrics before an album was released did not trouble him. Indeed, he felt real fans would still buy the album regardless of any downloads, even "just for the artwork."

Later, Stereophonics were one of several bands said to be involved in a ground-breaking agreement with Napster whereby the Association Of Independent Music announced they had signed an agreement for a worldwide licensing deal with Napster, allowing the entire catalogues of many artists to be posted on the Internet. Bands involved in this scheme also included Moby, Slipknot, Ash, Underworld, Tom Jones and Basement Jaxx.

Kelly also aired his views on the pop phenomenon that was Hear'Say, the band formed out of the hugely popular TV series *Pop Stars*. Kelly was said to have called them "soap stars" and was also credited with quotes such as "they shouldn't be allowed in the studio". One of the members of Hear'Say, fellow Welshman Noel Sullivan, reacted angrily to these comments attributed to Kelly, retaliating that, "I don't understand why he did it. We had real grief at the beginning from so-called proper bands. But we've done nothing different from them. We just did it in public, that's all. It's bang out of order." He went on to point out that other Welsh acts such as Cerys Matthews from Catatonia, Tom Jones, and even H from Steps had all been very helpful and supportive of his new band. He also spoke on the BBC about how "I'm really gutted that people I've looked up to have slated us because we're just having a go. They got their chance to have a go in their time. The next band who come after us, we're gonna applaud them!" Still, Kelly's views were shared by many music fans and the ultimate test was fast approaching - the Phonics new album release, at a time when Hear'Say's own debut long player was perched at Number 1 in the album charts. Not for long...

The Stereophonics' third album was released on April 9th, titled *Just Enough Education To Perform*. The phrase appeared in a lyric from the preceding single 'Mr Writer' and was actually taken from an old army reference book, originally being an army acronym for a 'general purpose' vehicle - Kelly's brother had actually written the phrase on his bedroom wall after a tour of duty in Northern Ireland. Kelly felt it was a fine title, because "it could mean so many different things. I think we all learn just enough in life to get by, and don't actually push ourselves to the extent we could." The album release was heralded by an ultra-exclusive gig at London's trendy Scala club in King's Cross. The show was a special for BBC Radio 1 and only a lucky 400 punters got hold of tickets for one of the most sought-after gigs of the year (the band returned to the Scala in September as part of *Q* magazine's 15th anniversary celebrations). On the actual day of the album's release, the band packed fans into the flagship HMV store in Oxford Street, London at midnight and Cardiff's Virgin Megastore at 4pm the same day.

Inadvertently, Stereophonics' new album had already attracted controversy before its release because of its proposed name. Originally, the band wanted to call the album *JEEP*, but enormo-brand Chrysler objected, saying they had trademarked this word for use with their automobiles. Kelly told one reporter how "We could have gone to court for it. But, you know, it's one thing to be controversial, but when somebody wants to go to a shop and buy a record and it's not there, controversial doesn't do anything for you." The artwork had to be re-made and this kept everyone busy as it was only six weeks before album release that the band opted to use the lengthier album title rather than the abbreviation.

Disappointing as this was for the band, the album itself was anything but an anticlimax for the legions of excited fans. The immediate observation was that the record was a mellower affair, no obvious fast-paced classic like 'Bartender'. At the same time, however, this reflected the band's altered lifestyles - the local vistas and scenarios of the first album and elements of the second had now been replaced by the rather controlled and yet more global spectrum that unavoidably imposes itself on any chart-topping band. Essentially, the effects of success had deprived Kelly of his parochial inspirations, replacing them with observations on the lifestyle he was now imbued with. After all, having toured almost relentlessly for years, it was inevitable that this would colour his focus.

Future single 'Vegas Two Times' was highly indicative of this. Held together by a searing riff - likened by many to an early Black Crowes B-side - the track complemented this rock edge with harmonised gospel vocals, a sure sign that the band were flexing their musical muscles. Lyrically, however, it does represent a good example of the more insular approach of this album. Hereafter, the music slows down and becomes decidedly melancholy.

Kelly has always enjoyed the paradox between a musically uplifting sound spread behind a very dour or dark theme - 'Local Boy' for example. The album's future summer smash single, 'Have A Nice Day' was another perfect example of this. Again inspired by a tour tale, the semi-acoustic song itself was a very moody embellishment of an experience they'd had after a gig at Slim's in San Francisco, as Kelly explained to one reporter: "There was a weird kind of taxi driver who was telling me that he hated tourists, and he couldn't understand why people come on holidays to surround themselves by other tourists. He said he was a poet and he was writing a poem called 'Corporate Communism,' which assumed that everybody in the world was exactly the same, apart from different accents. He said we all wear the same clothes and watch the same movies... and then he dropped us off and said, 'That'll be seven bucks. Have a nice day.' ..."I still don't know if I was paying for the story or for the actual ride." Yet, how Kelly chose to deliver this anecdote was via the summer's best slice of radio-friendly, uplifting pop-rock (which also happened to be his best vocal on the record).

This semi-acoustic flavour carries on with tracks such as 'Step on My Old Size Nines' and 'Lying in the Sun', marking a new-found confidence showing clearly that the wall of sound the Phonics were capable of, was not always necessary to deliver a killer track. Elsewhere, the lyrics were a little blunt - for example, the track 'Caravan Holidays' or the rather odd 'Every Day I Think of Money', but overall this was an astute and perceptive performance. It seems somewhat churlish to applaud a songwriter for his down-to-earth lyrics, watch enthusiastically as this success takes him a thousand miles from home and then be surprised and disappointed when his next lyrical output is not exclusively about the girl next door or the local dole queue.

Similarly, the record went musically further than the trio had ever ventured with extra vocals, gospel singers, slide guitars, authentic pianos and Wurlitzers. Kelly enthused to one writer how "it's not bigger, there's just a load more flavours on it. It's more dynamic as well, a free-sounding record that we can't wait to play live."

The rock mix was enterprising and refreshing, moving more towards Paul Weller than AC/DC and this bodes well for future Phonics albums. Despite some reviewers criticisms, it's hard to deny this was an extension of the breadth and depth of the Phonics songwriting and arranging. Overall, an accomplished record, a decided step forward - maybe not a reinvention of the wheel, but in the light of Oasis' dire *Standing On The Shoulder (sic) of Giants* and Blur and Radiohead's humourless (albeit critically fawned-over) drab offerings of late, the record was a welcome gesture. As writer Bill Aicher put it, "Stereophonics have finally come into their own (with) a truly mature disc (and) one that will inevitably propel them to the forefront of the minds of those who had previously ignored them."

Perhaps predictably after the lyrical content of 'Mr Writer', many parts of the press were a little tepid in their response to the new Phonics record.

Q magazine bemoaned the fact that in their opinion "for all the group's musical accomplishments, you (can't) help feeling that Jones was leading them to that place where rock groups prosaically sing about being in rock groups." The magazine went on to criticise the lyrics and the supposedly narrow subject matter. *Q* were not the lone sceptics but as the band had never been press darlings, this did not worry them at all.

Despite this often muted critical applause, the band's commercial strength was shown by the not unexpected news that *Just Enough Education To Perform* had entered the new charts at the top slot, misplacing the much-disliked Hear'Say. And so began a spell in the album charts that would last well into 2002. By August, just four months after release, *Just*

'There's just a load more flavours on the new record. It's more dynamic... a free-sounding record.'

Enough Education To Perform had gone double platinum, representing 600,000 units sold. Heading into the autumn, sales showed no signs of letting up and then before Christmas 2001, V Records announced they were re-releasing the album with bonus tracks and unusual formats. Although this drew complaints from some fans who had already purchased the record, the plan worked and the record soared back up the charts. Remarkably, in the New Year of 2002, the album re-took the Number 1 slot. Stereophonics status as the UK's premier band was now assured.

Of course, the album was supplemented by an array of excellent singles. The aforementioned 'Have A Nice Day' landed in the middle of summer at Number 5, (complete with Hendrix-inspired video with naked writhing ladies!), followed by the autumn arrival of the soft 'Step On My Old Size Nines', which also hit the Top Twenty. Interestingly, the Phonics did not promote this album quite so frantically as its predecessors and that was a deliberate policy on the band's part. They had, after all, worked the previous records with admirable application, but the experience had proved to be a very exhausting one. This time around, as Stuart explained to *The Calgary Sun*, they had decided to take things a little more slowly: "It was just a matter of figuring out how we want to work - it took us four or five years to figure that out because we were brand new in the industry and we didn't know how people worked. It has paid off and I think that's why we can slow down slightly." This more considered approach affected the success of the album not one iota - indeed, it probably added a frisson of mystique to the band's growing celebrity.

One area where the band seemed destined to have a continued battle is North America. Previous tour difficulties and illness had blighted earlier campaigns to 'break' the States. The February 2000 acoustic tours had been very well received but the scale was still small. For example, in Canada, which was the band's second biggest territory outside of the UK, *Just Enough Education To Perform* had sold only 14,000 copies by the time the same record had passed the one million mark in the UK. So, the band were excited about the prospect of returning to the continent to play the new record. The wider sound of the new album was supplemented by a second guitarist-singer, Scott James, and keyboardist Tony Kirkham for the purpose of touring. Kelly explained to *The Toronto Sun* that "I feel a lot of what we'd done in the past had been missed because of the volume of it. On the last album, even the quiet songs were loud - if that makes any sense. I like records where you can hear the band in a room. I think that's missing these days."

However, despite all the positive reactions to the new album and the band's eagerness to work it in the USA, the tour (which was due to begin in San Francisco in May and running through 11 dates to New York) had to be cancelled due to Kelly falling ill (he was advised by doctors to take a month off to recover from a chest infection caused by a serious bout of 'flu). The dates were provisionally realigned for September 2001, only to be cancelled yet again after the apocalyptic terrorist attacks of September 11th in New York and Washington. Immediately re-scheduling the shows for spring 2002, the band were admirably quick to point out that their musical careers were not important in this context, announcing that the cancellation was a mark of respect and sent their condolences to all affected.

Summer festival slots were played at T In The Park and for MTV as well as a 'virtual Glastonbury' set and a contribution to an Amnesty International 40th Anniversary show at Wembley Arena on 3rd June, 2001. Other acts performing here included Tom Jones, Badly Drawn Boy and Richard Blackwood. They also played their own headline European slots but the most prestigious shows that were fortunately not cancelled were the enormo-gigs supporting the biggest band in the world, U2. The Irish legends had arrived with their stunning new album, *All That You Can't Leave Behind* and instantly re-established themselves as rock gods, after a few odd records in the early 90s. Universal acclaim met their new record and Bono's status as pop icon and political figurehead for the 'Drop The Debt' campaign meant that this band were revered like perhaps no other in the new Millennium. Guitarist The Edge had seen the Phonics perform on Robbie Williams' bill at Slane Castle and promptly asked them to support his band on their forthcoming 'Elevation Tour' European and Scandinavian dates.

At these shows, the Phonics got on very well with U2, and gleaned advice from the 20 year veterans on how to handle the music business and all its pitfalls. As Kelly explained to one reporter, Bono's best pearl of wisdom was: "If you're going out for dinner four times a week and you look around the table and everybody's on your payroll, then you've probably become a prick."

The Stereophonics' live schedule in summer 2001 was, however, dominated by their own stadium concerts, originally pencilled in for Donnington Park Racetrack and Chepstow Racecourse. Reflecting the fact that the Phonics were one of the very few British bands who could sell this scale of show (Oasis, Prodigy etc), the gigs were announced in mid-March, 2001 and scheduled for July 14 and 21 respectively, under the banner of 'A Day At The Races'.

Initially, there were few signs of any difficulties, but that did not allow for the catastrophic foot and mouth crisis which had gripped British farmers since the spring. Kelly acknowledged that getting support bands for the two shows was hampered by most acts asking for too much money, since the traditional festivals were in jeopardy from the disease outbreak which saw animal pyres and mass culls for most of 2001. At first, the band said their own shows would probably not be in danger unless the government widened the limitations on outdoor events.

However, as the disease ran rampant across rural UK, the chances of the Chepstow gig being unaffected became increasingly slim until, in early April, it was announced that the band had been forced to cancel the show (all horse racing at that course was also cancelled). Remarkably, rather than leave just the one huge outdoor gig, the band quickly organised a monster show at none other than Cardiff's brand new, 72,000-seater Millennium Stadium (home to 1999's Manic Millennium concert and 2001's FA Cup Final). A recent outbreak of foot and mouth at a farm in Bayfield, Chepstow, just a mile from the original planned gig had put the final nail in the greenfield site's plans. Previously, the band had dubbed the two dates their 'foot and mouth tour.' The band issued a press statement which said, "We are naturally very disappointed that we have had to move the event but with the continuing progress of foot and mouth it became clear that bringing 60,000 people to a rural area was not in the best interests of the farming communities."

Once re-arranged, the two shows were a massive success. Just under 50,000 attended the Donnington Park show, while a further 55,000 crammed into the Millennium stadium. Supported was provided by Proud Mary, the Crocketts, Ash and finally The Black Crowes, who all primed the huge crowd perfectly for the main attraction. Kelly's first words when the Phonics arrived on stage to rapturous applause were "We're gonna start at the beginning" before launching into highlights from their debut album. A fairly chronological run through their greatest tracks was interjected with numbers such as the Rod Stewart cover, 'Lady Jane' (these shows later became available on DVD). The two hour gig at the Cardiff stadium was a replicate confirmation that the Phonics were now a major arena conquering outfit. Kelly could probably now stop worrying about any potential cauliflower wrapping...

Kelly's aforementioned reference to noise control as "missing these days" was a thinly veiled reference to the latest music phenomenon -

so-called American nu-metal. Initially ignited by the likes of Korn, the hard sound of nu-metal was taken to the masses by Fred Durst's Limp Bizkit, opening the door for a rash of similar bands to follow in his multi-platinum selling wake. Linkin Park, Alien Ant Farm, a revived The Offspring and even eventually the West Country's very own A enjoyed huge sales and popularity. The Phonics laid-back softer rock sound was the very antithesis of this fashion, but in a sense because the band's music had never been acutely fashionable in that sense, they never suffered when nu-metal was the craze. The Phonics success and popularity was now genuinely self-subsistent, a quality only a rare few bands can boast. Indeed, since September 11th, some observers had noticed that radio policy, particularly in America, was tending towards less aggressive music - just as the trend for all-action violent blockbuster films took a knock. More light-hearted, optimistic records were starting to be played and (for example) 'Have A Nice Day' slotted into that perfectly.

Back in the UK, the band continued with their all-conquering year. An arena tour in November had to be extended to cope with demand for tickets, a slew of awards from magazines and music television stations were squeezed into their ever-bulging cabinets and they even found time to contribute a cover of the Beatles' 'Don't Let Me Down' to the soundtrack for the forthcoming blockbuster, *I Am Sam*, starring Sean Penn and Michelle Pfeiffer. The movie centres around a mentally backward man who is obsessed with the Fab Four, hence the soundtrack of Beatles songs by the likes of Sarah McLachlan, The Wallflowers, Eddie Vedder, Nick Cave and The Vines.

Continuing with their interest in covers, the band released a new single in late November 2001, the fabulous 'Handbags And Gladrags' (previous B-sides including The Rolling Stones' 'Angie', The Beatles' 'I'm Only Sleeping' and Nirvana's 'Something In The Way' had never been A-side singles). The track was, as previously pointed out, a Mike D'Abo song, but it was Rod Stewart's version taken from his 1970 debut solo album *An Old Raincoat Won't Ever Let You Down*, that had enjoyed perhaps the biggest impact. The track had been used live during all of the various acoustic shows (both UK and USA) and was then re-recorded by the band earlier in 2001 with Jools Holland And His Rhythm And Blues Orchestra.

The oboe-led classic was perhaps the most direct comparison between Kelly and Rod Stewart and, with the aid of the performance video, the single enjoyed huge advance airplay and MTV-time. Not surprisingly, it entered the chart at Number 4, helped by the intriguing B-side of 'First Time Ever I Saw Your Face' (which was written by Ewan Maccoll, and famously performed by Roberta Flack). Impressively, almost three months later the single was still in the Top 30. This was partly helped by the massive cult success of the UK's finest new comedy since *The Royal Family*, namely Ricky Gervais' masterpiece of spoof documentary, *The Office*. The fly-on-the-wall sitcom also used a version of 'Handbags And Gladrags' and such was its popularity that thousands more copies of the Phonics rendition were sold as the 'soundtrack'. The *NME* even ran an article asking people if they had heard the Welsh band's version first, or if they had seen the comedy show first. Either way, it boosted the single and led the Phonics into the New Year with yet another slice of acclaim and commercial success. 'Handbags...' was one of the bonus tracks which, at Christmas 2001, was included on the aforementioned re-release of *Just Enough Education To Perform*.

Unfortunately, 2002 did not start off well at all for some of the band's friends - they were shocked to hear in January that Feeder's drummer, Jon Lee, had committed suicide at his Miami home, leaving behind a wife and young son. Kelly told the press how "it's just a big shock really, it's unbelievable, it's horrible news... it's tragic. I was talking to the guy just before Christmas and he was excited about going home to see his family."

Meanwhile, the band had a hectic January already penned in - almost a round the world trip in 25 days! Starting off in Japan's Nagoya before moving through much of the USA and then Canada, the band's relentless approach to gigging had clearly not been blunted. Kelly told one newspaper how they viewed the task abroad: "You just got to go to these places and try to prove your point. There's a million bands out there trying to do something, but I believe that we're doing some songs that can touch people. That's what we've done in this country, so I'm sure we can do it everywhere else." This time, Stuart was absent from some of these dates ("due to family reasons") but met up again with the rest of the group in

Los Angeles (Owen Hopkin of The Crocketts drummed in Stuart's temporary absence). These dates would then be complemented by an extensive European tour in March 2002, visiting Holland, France and Italy.

In keeping with their status as perhaps the UK's biggest band to be regularly snubbed, the Phonics had a 'disagreement' with the Brit Award organisers in early 2002. They had been nominated for 'Best British Band' and *Just Enough* was the previous year's biggest selling album by a British act, yet the trio were not invited to perform at the February 20 ceremony at Earl's Court in London. Rumours abounded the Brit organisers wanted an American guitar band instead and, completely understandably, Kelly was not impressed. He explained to one writer how, "We've never really had any praise from anything having to do with the British music industry - whether it be press or TV shows. We've always been the underdog or odd one out kinda thing. The whole Brits ceremony is set up for people to sell more records". In a vain attempt to pacify the angered Welshmen, the Brits then suggested they perform 'Handbags' with Rod Stewart, which it seemed only added insult to injury as Kelly explained: "We turned down the thing with Rod Stewart because we didn't want to play a collaboration set, we wanted to do our own songs. Everything we've achieved has been off our own back, same thing with 'Handbags And Gladrags' - it had nothing to do with Rod Stewart. I love The Faces and everything Rod Stewart did in the 70s, but it's not something we'd like to do right now."

Despite this furore, the future still looks very rosy indeed for the Phonics. Another single from the smash album *J.E.E.P* will surface in early April - 'Vegas Two Times' (which will also be the first Phonics single to be made available on the DVD format including tonnes of audio-visual features). They are reputed to be wanted to play at the Jubilee concerts for the Queen and at the re-launched Isle of Wight festival. Kelly is still working on developing his script which is said to be centred in the 1940s around the life of Albert Pierrepoint, one of Britain's last hangmen, who worked before the abolition of capital punishment in 1965. Both Billy Connolly and Rhys Ifans are rumoured to have expressed interest in the project. Kelly also collaborated on the song 'What Do You Think?' with Rolling Stone Ronnie Wood for the latter's new album, *Not For Beginners*, which also was to feature work with Bob Dylan, Ian McLagan, Ron's son Jessie and his daughter Leah.

As for their new album, the band had quite a large pot of ideas already being mulled over by spring 2002. 'Handbags' had inspired Kelly: "I've learned so much, just by the result we've had and the reaction from those songs that we did in such a kind of spontaneous way. I'm definitely going to take that on board on the next record." Plans are to begin recording in autumn 2002 with a 2003 release tentatively pencilled in.

Stereophonics are now established in the upper echelons of British rock music and with the huge commercial success of *J.E.E.P* now behind them, the anticipation for their next musical outing is already developing. As usual, it is Stuart who articulates the most grounded review of their long, frantic and incredible journey, as he told *Q* magazine: "There are worse ways to earn a living, like working on a building site or fitting PVC windows and doors - which is what I'd probably be doing otherwise..." Kelly is equally modest: "We are just starting out, still trying to figure out who we are, where we're going to go." Looking back at the Phonics career to date, with all its multiple twists and surprising turns, who knows indeed, but it will certainly be fascinating to watch...

DISCOGRAPHY

SINGLES

LOOKS LIKE CHAPLIN
More Life In A Tramp's Vest

Limited Edition
Double A-Side Single;
Release Date November 1996
V2 Records SPH-D1

LOCAL BOY IN
THE PHOTOGRAPH
Too Many Sandwiches
Buy Myself A Small Plane

Release Date March 1997
V2 Records SPH-D2
Highest Chart Position No. 51

MORE LIFE IN
A TRAMP'S VEST

CD1:
Raymond's Shop
Poppy Day

CD2:
Looks Like Chaplin
Too Many Sandwiches
Last Of The Big Time Drinkers
(All recorded live for Radio 1
March 1997)

Release Date May 1997
V2 Records SPH-D4
Highest Chart Position No. 33

A THOUSAND TREES

CD1:
Carrot Cake And Wine
A Thousand Trees (Recorded
live for Radio 1 March 1997)

CD2:
Home To Me
Looks Like Chaplin,
Summertime
(Four-song acoustic EP)

Release Date 11 August 1997
V2 Records VVR500443/8
Highest Chart Position No. 22

TRAFFIC

CD1:
Tie Me Up Tie Me Down
Coal Chambers

CD2:
More Life In A Tramp's Vest
A Thousand Trees
Local Boy In The Photograph
(Recorded live at the Belfort
Festival, July 1997)

Release Date 27 October 1997
V2 Records VVR500943/8
Highest Chart Position No. 20

LOCAL BOY IN
THE PHOTOGRAPH
Re-Issue

CD1:
Who'll Stop The Rain
Check My Eyelids For Holes
Local Boy In The
Photograph (Video)

CD2:
Not Up To You
(Recorded live for XFM),
The Last Resort
Traffic (Video)

Release Date 9 February 1998
V2 Records VVR501263/8
Highest Chart Position No. 14

**THE BARTENDER AND
THE THIEF**

CD1:
She Takes Her Clothes Off
Fiddlers Green

CD2:
Traffic
Raymond's Shop (All recorded
live at Cardiff Castle)

Release Date 9 November 1998
V2 Records VVR501263/8
Highest Chart Position No. 3

JUST LOOKING

CD1:
Postmen Do Not Make Great
 Movie Heroes
Sunny Afternoon

CD2:
Local Boy In The Photograph
Same Size Feet (Both recorded
live for Radio 1)

Release Date 22 February 1999
V2 Records VVR501263/8
Highest Chart Position No. 4

**PICK A PART
THAT'S NEW**

CD1:
Nice To Be Out
Positively Fourth Street,
Pick A Part That's New
(Video)

CD2:
Pick A Part That's New
(Acoustic Version)
In My Day
Something In The Way

Release Date 3 May 1999
V2 Records VVR 5006773/8
Highest Chart Position No. 4

**I WOULDN'T
BELIEVE YOUR RADIO**

CD1:
The Bartender And The Thief
(Bar Version)
The Old Laughing Lady

CD2:
Pick A Part That's New
T-Shirt Suntan (All recorded
live at Morfa, July 1999)

Release Date 23 August 1999
V2 Records VVR 5008823/8
Highest Chart Position No. 11

HURRY UP AND WAIT
CD1:
Hurry Up and Wait (Single
Version)
Angie
I Wouldn't Believe Your Radio

CD2: (Enhanced)
Hurry Up and Wait*
I Stopped To Fill My Car Up*

Billy Daveys Daughter*
Hurry Up and Wait**

*Recorded Live at Morfa
Stadium; **live footage from
Morfa

Release Date 8th November 1999
V2 Records VVR5009323
Highest Chart Position No. 11

MR WRITER
CD1:
Mr Writer (Edit)
Maritim Belle Vue In Kiel
An Audience with Mr Nice

CD2:
Mr Writer (Acoustic version)
Hurry Up And Wait (Acoustic
Version)
Don't Let Me Down (Acoustic
Version) All the above are live.

Release Date March 2001
V2 Records VVR5015933
Highest Chart Position No. 5

HAVE A NICE DAY
CD1:
Have a Nice Day
Surprise
Piano for a Stripper

CD2:
Have a Nice Day (Live at
Birmingham Irish Centre)
Heart of Gold (Live at York
Grand Opera House)
I Stoppped to Fill My Car Up
(Live at Birmingham Irish
Centre)

Release Date June 2001
V2 Records VVR5016243
Highest Chart Position No. 5

DISCOGRAPHY

STEP ON MY OLD SIZE NINES

CD1:
Step On My Old Size Nines
Shoeshine Boy
I'm Only Sleeping
Step On My Old Size Nines (video)

CD2:
Step On My Old Size Nines
Everyday I Think Of Money
I'm Just Looking

Release Date September 2001
V2 Records VVR5016253
Highest Chart Position No. 16

HANDBAGS AND GLADRAGS

CD1:
Handbags and Gladrags
First Time Ever I Saw Your Face
How

CD2:
Handbags and Gladrags (live acoustic)
Caravan Holiday (live acoustic)
Nice To Be Out (live acoustic)

Release Date December 2001
V2 Records VVR5017753
Highest Chart Position No. 5

VEGAS TWO TIMES

CD:
Vegas Two Times (album version),
Mr Writer (live), Watch Them Fly
Sundays (live)

DVD:
Audio: Vegas Two Times (radio
edit), Vegas Two Times (live), Roll
Up And Shine (live) Videos of Vegas
Two Times, clips of Mr Writer,
Watch Them Fly Sundays, Step On
My Old Size Nines, Local Boy In
The Photograph (all live), lyric
screen, photo gallery and wallpaper.

Release Date 1st April 2002
V2 Records

ALBUMS

WORD GETS AROUND

A Thousand Trees
Looks Like Chaplin
More Life In A Tramp's Vest
Local Boy In The Photograph
Traffic
Not Up To You
Check My Eyelids For Holes
Same Size Feet
Last Of The Big Time Drinkers
Goldfish Bowl
Too Many Sandwiches
Billy Davey's Daughter

Release Date 25 August 1997
V2 Records VVR1000438
Highest Chart Position Number 6

PERFORMANCE AND COCKTAILS

Roll Up And Shine
The Bartender And The Thief
Hurry Up And Wait
Pick A Part That's New
Just Looking
Half The Lies You Tell Ain't True
I Wouldn't Believe Your Radio
T-Shirt Suntan
Is Yesterday Tomorrow Today?
A Minute Longer
She Takes Her Clothes Off
Plastic California
I Stopped To Fill My Car Up

Release Date 8 March 1999
V2 Records VVR1000438
Highest Chart Position Number 1

JUST ENOUGH EDUCATION TO PERFORM

Vegas Two Times
Lying In The Sun
Mr. Writer
Step On My Old Size Nines
Have A Nice Day
Nice To Be Out
Watch Them Fly Sundays
Everyday I Think Of Money
Maybe
Caravan Holiday
Rooftop

Release Date 9th April 2001
V2 Records VVR1015832
Highest Chart Position Number 1
(Extended Album Version Also Available